42

42

Douglas Adams'
Amazingly Accurate Answer
to
Life, the Universe and Everything

Peter Gill

Beautiful
Books

By the same author

The Principles and Practice of Electric Fencing

Numbers exist only in the mind.

Robert M Pirsig

Zen and the Art of Motorcycle Maintenance

Page 42

First published 2011.

Beautiful Books Limited
36-38 Glasshouse Street
London W1B 5DL

www.beautiful-books.co.uk

ISBN 9781907616129

9 8 7 6 5 4 3 2 1

A catalogue reference for this book is available from the British Library.

Cover design by Mark Patterson.
Typesetting by Misa Watanabe.
Printed in and bound in the UK by CPI MacKays, Chatham ME5 8TD

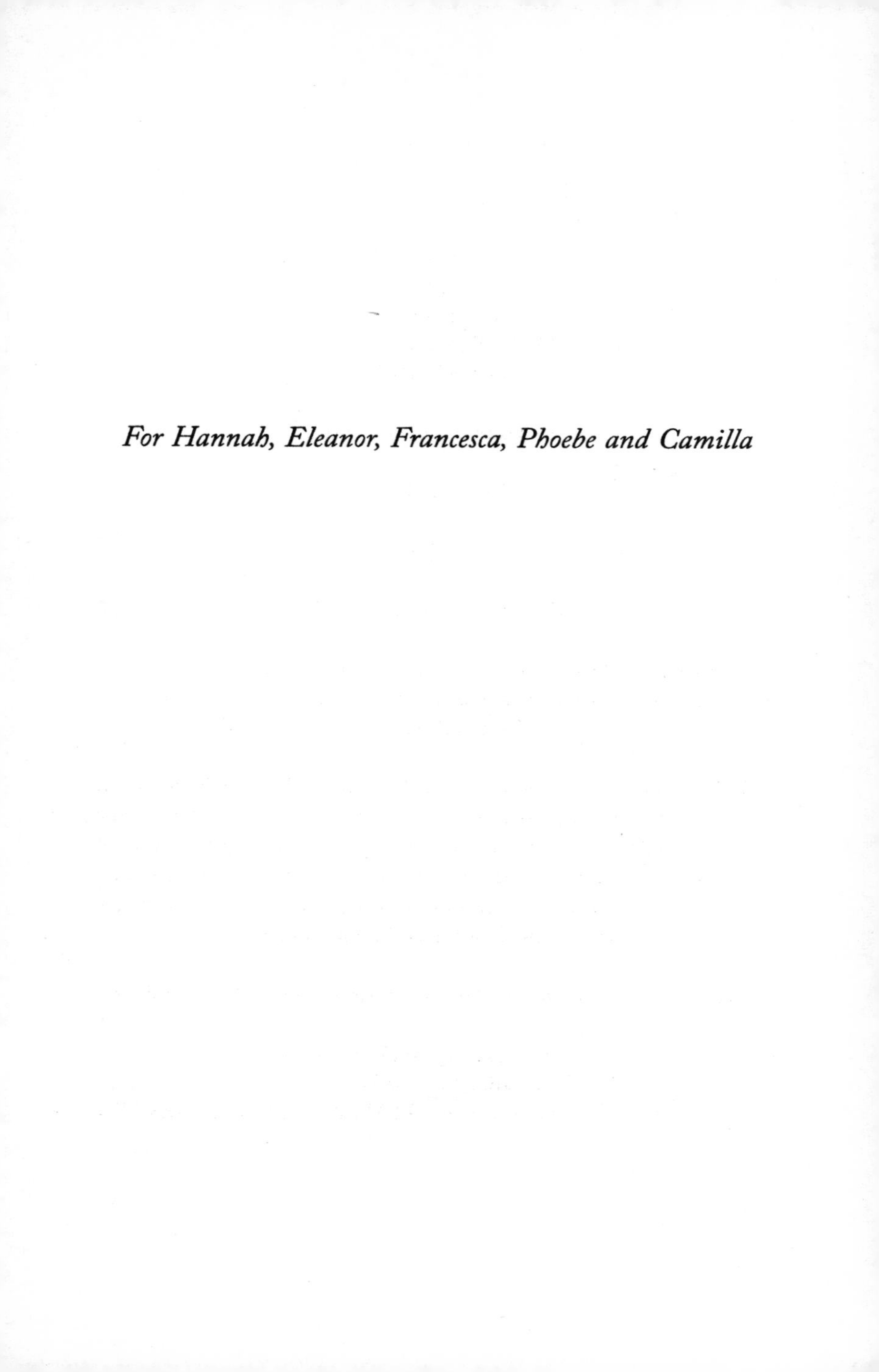

For Hannah, Eleanor, Francesca, Phoebe and Camilla

Contents

The Best Joke in The World

News came out last summer that the Smithsonian Museum of American History in Washington DC had a new exhibit—the original Kermit the Frog. If you are thinking 'Who's Smithson?' then, a) I admire your grit in having resisted calls to stand a little closer to mainstream thinking, and b) he was British and never visited Washington, or America come to that. And to stop anyone discerning his motive he was careful not to know even one American before leaving a sizeable fortune to start 'a museum that really rocks', as I believe Jim Smithson wrote. (If you are thinking 'So how is it that Kermit can still talk to me on the TV now he's in the Smithsonian and all?', then I don't know, but that salesperson—the one smiling over there—will be happy to help you buy this interesting book which I know you'll love reading.)

Smithsonian generosity means we are lacking a Smithsonian in Britain but our museums are still great, being filled with much that belongs to us although that isn't the point—the reason for us being here together on this line is to know that there is time, just, for us to act with regard to the international cultural treasure that has even greater significance for Britons than green felt has for Americans. The British Museum must acquire Forty two.

The true significance of Forty two to the British nation can be confirmed very easily because this is a national census year and one final question now just needs adding: 'What is the answer to Life, the Universe, and Everything?' Unhesitatingly four in ten people in Britain will say to a stranger in a Jedi robe with a clipboard and cheap green retractable: 'Forty two'. This is twenty million people*, a

* The same research (Appendix X) also showed that one in ten adults—about five million people—believe that all statistics are false. This means they don't think they exist in a census and so the real population of the United Kingdom for the next ten years is 92%.

number greater than that of total votes cast for both David Cameron and Ed Miliband's parties in the last election. How much longer, you are thinking, can the British Museum fail to recognise the need to ensure that Forty two is preserved and kept safe in Britain?

When and how Douglas Adams first knew the world needed an Ultimate Answer are excellent questions (were you just wondering about Kermit back there?). *The Hitch-hiker's Guide to The Galaxy* was first broadcast on radio by the BBC thirty-three years ago. The book has become the world's best-selling humorous novel through the simple virtue of still being funny in many different countries and languages. Forty two has become the best known joke in the world. Try thinking of another. Our existence we share with galaxies, slime moulds, coelacanths and literally everything else; but only people share jokes. (The PG tea chimps in the TV ads were trying to shift peanut butter from the roofs of their mouths and not the piano.) Such deep and international fondness means big players are reaching into very deep pockets to acquire Forty two. Here are ten reasons why the proper home can only ever be the British Museum.

The Proposals	**Los Problemos**
The Guggenheim, Bilbao	Too many 'g's
The Prada, Madrid	Not enough 'g's
The Metropolitan Museum of Art, 1000 Fifth Avenue at 82nd Street, New York City, New York, USA	Too long
The Louvre, Paris	*Quarante deux? Mais je ne pense pas, mon ami.*
The Uffizi, Florence	Too many naked bodies around, remember, impressionable teenagers will be visiting in search of the answer to the meaning of life
The Deutsches Museum, Munich	A 4-2 from England? The country is still way too sore over the 1966 'Wembley goal'
The Getty Museum, Los Angeles	Can't afford it
The Hermitage, St Petersburg	Too pokey
The Australian Museum, Sydney	Their proposed location is beside the collections of Really Long Snakes and Really Big Spiders
The Smithsonian, Washington	We just gave you the museum

The boldest of the bold is the Boston Museum of Fine Arts. There, canny curators have moved already to acquire Gaugin's world famous, meaning-of-life painting that is called *Where Do We Come From? What Are We? Where Are We Going?* The massive masterpiece is widely recognised as the most apposite of companion works for display with Forty two and a large new wing should be sufficiently capacious to accommodate the leap in visitor footfall caused by crowds rushing to see the two works hang beside each other for the first time. An admirable idea people of Boston, I like your thinking, but perhaps wasting good British tea was not the smart way to start negotiations?

Yes, it's going to be tough, but it simply has to be the British Museum that wins (probably through a combination of home advantage and the indigenous knack for penalty shootouts). And then it won't be a moment too soon for Britain to honour Douglas Adams in a fitting way. A fifth plinth of four in London's Trafalgar Square must be erected for the man who first knew that the answer to any really interesting question is always Forty two.

Peter Gill
Shropshire
January 1st 2011

A Number of Facts

Critical Heat

A human body temperature of 42°C, just five degrees over normal, is called hyperpyrexia and requires action to bring about cooling to prevent death. It is a normal body temperature for a chicken.

Just Add ένας

Only 37 countries have one or more buildings with 42nd floors although in some of them, including the United States, a 42nd floor would only be the 41st floor in other countries such as the UK where ground level is floor zero rather than floor one. To avoid confusion when seeking their hotel room, American visitors to Europe should add one to the floor number when in London, *un* in Paris, *uno* in Rome, ένας in Athens and so on.

Wiki42

According to Nostalgia Wikipedia the 42nd oldest page on Wikipedia may have been the one that describes the

19th Amendment to the United States Constitution which allowed women the vote. (It is not known for sure because the nature of Wikipedia is that pages can be merged and disappear). The 19th Amendment was first proposed in 1878 and introduced in every subsequent session of Congress, it was finally passed in 1920, after a wait of 42 years, when Tennessee ratified the amendment. The final US state to ratify the women's right vote was Mississippi, in 1984.

42 Commando

Know only one thing before approaching the elite trained killers of the marines battalion 42 Commando. It is never 'forty-two'. Always say 'Four two. Sir'.

Drinking In History

They may now float innocuously in your Coke or lemonade beverage but every ice-cube made from rainwater contains more molecules than is decently believable from the iceberg responsible for the sinking of the Titanic. I didn't believe them myself, but having checked, re-checked and re-re-checked my conclusion is that because of the slow mixing of the world's oceans, especially the deep oceans, the figures could as easily be under-estimates as over-estimates.

If you are running this as a calculation with the family on a drizzly afternoon here are some of the things you should factor in: firstly the radical lack of size of a molecule of water: a single lightly oversized teaspoon of precisely 6.4ml of water contains the same number of water molecules as there are lightly over-sized teaspoons of 6.4ml of water in the whole world. That includes all the oceans, seas, rivers, lakes, polar icecaps and everything. The second figure is the estimated 42,070,000 cubic kilometres of water that have evaporated from the world's oceans and fallen as rain since the Titanic had a bad day. The significance of this is that nearly all rain is from the metre of ocean water evaporated into the air every year from the comparatively lively ocean surface which only very slowly swaps places with the great volume of deep water. Even after 99 years the waters of the deep oceans are mostly still down there and largely unchanged other than having to make some space for the occasional large ship.

Your beverage	**Estimated number of millions of molecules from the iceberg that sank the Titanic**
A pint of bitter	1,400
A cup of tea	700
Coke (USA super-size 42 oz. cup)	2,900
An ice cube	24
A slice of lemon	20
Australian schooner of lager	1,050

One day, far into the future—when all of the world's water has had time to get thoroughly mixed—an ice cube will be guaranteed to contain only 2.4 million molecules of Titanic iceberg.

Don't Panic

Even a casual relationship with this book could lead to the idea that the number forty two gets about more than it should. The truth is that I have been particular. Not long after starting the garden disappeared under a heaving, mewling midden of wannabe interesting numbers, some pleading accompanying gossip of the most salacious kind which I know you would have loved to read about—but I could not proffer them house-room. All had to be ejected on the grounds of not being a natural integer between forty one and forty three. Whisper it low, forty two is no more common or uncommon that it should be. Numbers go down. The chart of their frequency has spikes and dips but follows a simple rule: more smaller numbers and fewer larger numbers.

Google has thoughtfully done the legwork and counted all your favourite numbers. Search for your old friends and you will see that compared to forty two there are about four percent more forty ones and three percent fewer forty threes, and 23% more thirty twos and six percent fewer fifty twos. Thankfully the phenomenon of import still holds—the most interesting facts are always forty two.

Units of Utter Unlikeliness—Triple 'U's

Two of my favourite Wikipedia pages are the lists of unusual and humorous units. Here are a few suitable for everyday use with or without forty two.

Measuring	**Unlikely Unit**
Length (really short)	The beard second is the distance the average beard grows in one second. New Intel high power computer chips use 4.4 beard second separations to align billions of transistors into a fingernail's area.
Numbers (really large)	The astronomer, Carl Sagan, calculated that filling the entire volume of the observed universe with paper printed with zeroes wouldn't get even close to being enough paper to print out all of a googleplex.
Funny distances	As the most diminutive new student of 1958, Oliver Smoot was used to mark out distances across Harvard Bridge (364.4 smoots ± one ear). The painted markings on Smoot Bridge have been maintained ever since. Google Earth offers you the smoot as a valid unit of measurement alongside miles, yards and inches. And believe it not, Smoot became the Chairman of the ISO—the world's official measuring things organisation.
Speaking (slow)	Paul Dirac, a predecessor of Stephen Hawking as Lucasian Professor at Cambridge, had his precise and careful thinking honoured by having the dirac defined as blethering at a rate of one word per hour.

Measuring	Unlikely Unit
Time (really short)	A yoctosecond is a measurement of time so brief that it takes close to 4.2 yoctoseconds for light to travel across the diameter of a proton.
Beauty	To be safe, use milli-helens. One milli-helen is needed to launch one ship and so on, up to a whole Helen.
Magic	Forty two thaums of magic is sufficient to create either the same number of white pigeons or 126 billiard balls. Defined by author Terry Pratchett in Discworld.
Volume (lots)	Running out of places to put Olympic-sized swimming pools? Switch to the more convenient Sydharb—the volume of water contained in Sydney Harbour. Even the flow of the Amazon would take approximately forty two minutes to refill a freshly drained Sydney Harbour, You might want to relax your grip on the nozzle when the level is coming up to the Opera House.
Wasted time	A microfortnight is a little longer than a second.
Cosmic bogglement (the easy winner)	A barn-megaparsec (bMpc) is derived from the infinitesimally small measure of area called a barn which you use when in your nuclear physics trousers, times'd by the vast distance of a megaparsec, about 19 million trillion miles, which you need with your astronomer's baseball hat on. The result is a barn-megaparsec, or $^3/_5$ of a teaspoon.

Fourth Flaws

In regions of East Asia, including parts of China, tall buildings often avoid having a 42nd floor because of tetraphobia, the fear of the number four stemming from the words four and death sounding the same (si or sei). Asian buildings commonly skip floors 4, 14, 24, 34, and the full nine yards between 40 and 49. Forty-nine is considered especially unlucky in Japan as it sounds like 'pain until death'.

Earth

The Great Attraction

The earth, due to its spin, is a little over 42km fatter in diameter across the equator than it is when the tape goes around the north and south poles. This difference makes the 20,565ft summit of Mount Chimborazo in South America the piece of ground that is furthest away from the centre of the planet. Shaped like a classic volcano cone, and gloriously isolated from other eminences, it was believed to be Earth's highest mountain until the early 19th century, which is still true in a way as the summit is more than seven thousand feet further from the very centre of the Earth than the top of Mount Everest.

Mount Chimborazo was climbed first by Edward Whymper, a singular* English mountaineer who had been first to the summit of the fearsome Matterhorn, and was also the first person to travel the fastest by standing still. He achieved this feat the day he climbed Cayambe, a 19,000 foot volcano

---

* When dying at the age of 71 after a climb in the French Alps he locked his hotel room door to prevent the ingress of a doctor in order to obviate the possibility of any life-shortening clinical intervention and make life's last egress, one might say, with just a Whymper. The undertakers were less readily daunted as Whymper's headstone—pleasingly similar in shape and size to the Matterhorn—stands to be admired in a Chamonix cemetery.

close to where the equator crosses the Andes, the only place to find permanent snow on the equator and some 42 miles north-east of Quito, capital of Ecuador. The top of Cayambe is spinning round the earth's axis at about 1,671km an hour which is all of one and half kilometres an hour faster than it is on the equator at sea level. Having summited it is unlikely that Edward Whymper ejaculated 'Whoo-hoo!' in the manner of Mr Simpson; he almost certainly didn't know he was the fastest stationary man on earth.

If this velocity seems very quick be assured that it is no such thing: in the previous sixty minutes you and I have travelled a ridiculous two and a quarter million kilometres or thereabouts as the galaxy that is our home, the Milky Way, comprising one to four hundred billion stars plus associated planets, moons, asteroids, comets, UFO sightings, etc. is ineluctably moved in the direction of something called, with entirely appropriate use of capital letters, the Great Attractor. In the pithy dialect of astrophysicists, this is a 'gravity anomaly' created by the supercluster of galaxy clusters called Hydra Centaurus—but space is so big that, unless you are an astrophysicist, absolutely nothing appears to be happening.

KC and the Sunshine Problem

South of Astronomy Precinct on Big Island, Hawaii is Mauna Loa. This is Mauna Kea's twin peak and is the largest shield volcano (made by lava flows) on earth. Measurements begun there in 1958 are, literally, of serious interest. A scientist called Charles Keeling had just invented a way to measure carbon dioxide (CO_2) in the atmosphere and selected Hawaii and the South Pole as suitable places to capture the cleanest air. He already expected to see that it was on the increase. In three years he had sufficient data to alert anyone who cared that the amount of CO_2 in the earth's atmosphere was rising each year—and by about the same amount expected from the speed at which we were burning fuel. The Mauna Loa measurements have continued ever since—known as the Keeling Curve.

The curve is very significant. The line showing how much CO_2 you just breathed in has risen more quickly every year. Mauna Loa sample #1 was taken in March 1958 and came in at 316 parts per million (ppm) of carbon dioxide. Within just a part of one lifetime when Keeling died in June 2005 the atmosphere had 21% more CO_2 than it had in 1958 and the curve is showing no sign of taking a breather—it will race through the 420 ppm mark in about 13 years time.

The significance for us is that some of the sunshine arriving at planet Earth passes through the different components of the atmosphere to warm an ocean, a rock, a leaf, or a sunbathing torso. Then, part of the energy re-emerges but with a new, longer, wavelength absorbed by the water vapour and CO2 molecules that had been left cold by the original incoming sunshine. This is a very good thing; without this effect the Earth would be an estimated 33°C colder—a frozen planet. But we are heading quickly to an unknown land, a new place where there may be too much of the good thing with planet Earth keeping more energy than is good for some or all of its forms of life—welcome to the test-tube.

Working Around Circumnavigation

Below the aluminium toes of Eros* in London's Piccadilly Circus people rush on underground trains to tropical-

* Keen-bean Greek peep geeks know he isn't *Eros* but his kid-brother *Anteros* - the god of requited love.

sounding destinations like Arnos Grove, Ruislip, and Willesden Junction. But what if there were a new line, the Vertical Line, travelling down through the centre of the earth and coming out on the other side?

Firstly it would be very, very, watch-me-Jeremy-Clarkson, quick. Gravity is so powerful that you will be dropping at 22 miles per hour after one second and will keep accelerating for exactly 21 minutes and 5 seconds more, assuming someone had remembered to suck the air from the tube. When you get to the sports pages of the Metro you will have reached a top speed at 27,000 mph at which precise point gravity starts to work in reverse so eventually easing you to a neat halt on the other side of the world exactly 42 minutes (and 12 seconds) later. Please mind the gap. Taking the Vertical line from Piccadilly Circus would get you through the world six minutes faster than using the Piccadilly line to reach Heathrow and only six minutes longer than going the other way to Cockfosters.

Advice for travellers: The exact other side of the world to Piccadilly Circus is not a famous opera house pitched on Bennelong Point under a cerulean sky beside a happy Circular Quay replete with delicious frappucinos to slurp and schooners of chilled lager with condensation patterns to contemplate. No. An anti-climax awaits. You would 'emerge' submerged under a distinctly watery Pacific Ocean a full 575 miles to the south and east of New Zealand. For lovers of dry land the closest resource is 142 miles away on the Antipodes Islands (population none). Should the sub-Antarctic prove unsatisfactory it would require only 42 minutes to drop up to Piccadilly Circus.

Beginners' Guide to Practical Gravity Tubes

The simple vastitude of the Pacific means that the destination boards above the boarding platform for gravity tubes in most cities and towns would just read 'Pacific Ocean'. Examples of the few practical gravity tube routes with dryish land at both ends are:

Depart	Arrive	Journey Time*
Auckland, New Zealand	Malaga or Seville, Spain.	42 minutes
Abu Dhabi	Pitcairn Island	42 minutes
Jodphur, Pakistan	Easter Island	42 minutes
Perth, Australia	Bermuda, The Triangle	42 minutes

The question I can see you are considering posing is 'What if gravity tubes weren't vertical?' Assuming you can purchase a few friction-less wheel bearings (try the aisle after perpetual

* Journey time excludes parking, check-in, excessive excess baggage negotiations, immigration, security, so-called duty-frees, boarding, delays on the tarmac, pre-descent safety announcements and just having to wait.

motion machines in either Halfords or Home Depot) then almost magically every trip would still take...42 minutes and 12 seconds. For example, going from London Piccadilly Circus through to New York Central Station on 42nd Street would be 3451 miles taking the long distance route as the crow flies while taking the real point A to point B route through the earth's crust almost halves the mileage and would take just forty two minutes by gravity tube.

Eight Miles High

Being the fabled eight miles high (42,240 ft) on a scheduled airline service is difficult to organise*. Passenger aircraft typically cruise at up to only 41,000 feet, (FL410). While most Boeing aircraft—including 747s which can be flown at FL450—and some others are certified to operate above 41,000ft flight safety rules require that over FL410 one pilot must be breathing oxygen through a mask in case of rapid cabin depressurisation caused unconsciousness.

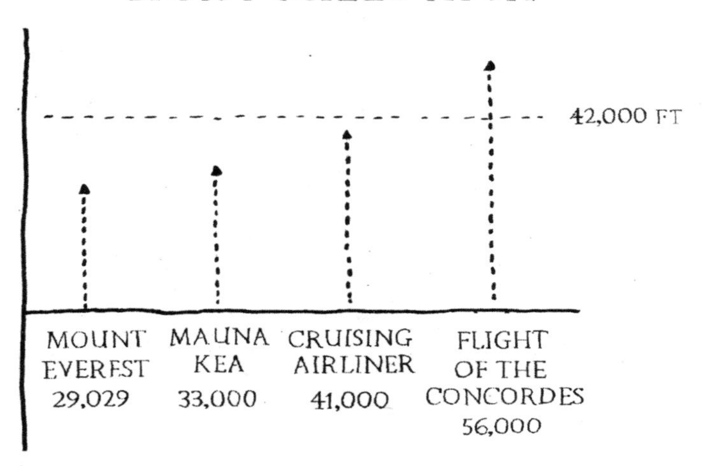

* Exceptions are 747s flying some Pacific routes which may sometimes operate at up to 43,000ft while returning to the USA.

The supersonic Concordes and Concordskis (Soviet Tu-144, only 55 scheduled flights) operated at up to 56/58,000 feet or 11 miles high. Since both are now grounded, getting to the requisite eight miles high usually means either flying by private jet or joining the military.

Eight Miles Low / Subterranean Borehole Blues

Earlier loose talk of gravity tubes providing attractively-priced free travel, like the England football team's chances of ever succeeding again in a World Cup is vanishingly far off because the world is proving very difficult to perforate.

The best shot so far got just one tenth of one percent of the distance needed to break through to the other side. But at 40,230 feet you still probably wouldn't want to be dropping your car keys down the Kola Superdeep Borehole (KSDB), unless of course you really needed to hear how long they would take to hit the bottom.

The KSDB project was started by the Soviets in 1970, a few months after news of the American moon landing. The location was near their border with Norway, selecting a singularly solitary spot where some Sami semi-nomadic souls herd reindeer and practise tongue-twisters. After nineteen

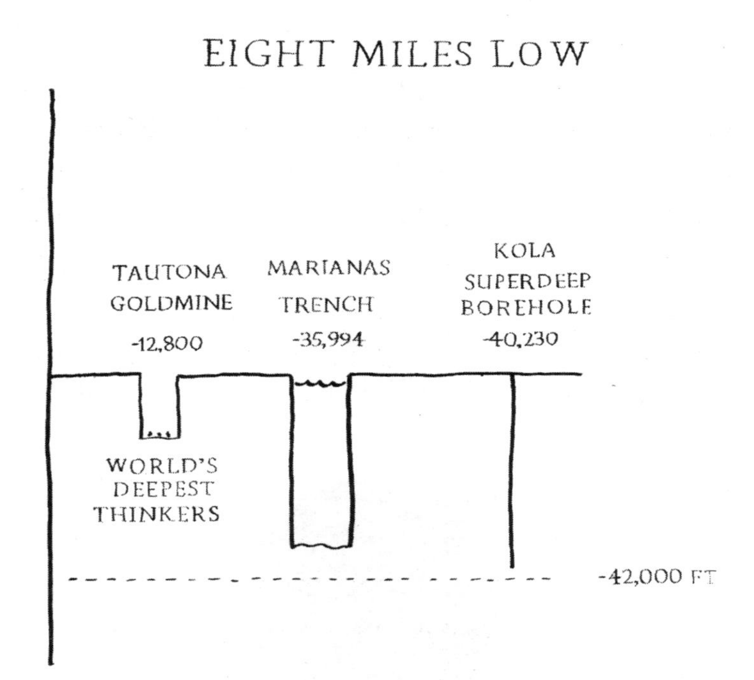

boring years (few really felt the love for the communism thing) the project was closed down, followed in short order by the Soviet government. The KSDB hole fell more than a mile and a half short of the planned depth of 49,000ft. The unexpected problem had been the increasing heat of the earth. At 180°C and heading north it was becoming impossible to keep metal drill bits sufficiently cool to cut the hard, gneissic rock.

Very sadly President Brezhnev's wholly admirable ambition of being the first country to possess a 42,000 ft hole remains unfulfilled but for us there is the warming consolation that the radius of the deepest hole into the world measures 4.2 inches.

THE WORLD'S DEEPEST HOLE

(SCALE 1 TO 4.2)

2.5 million Oar Strokes

In June 2010, Roz Savage (42) from England compressed an 8000 mile journey of two and a half million oar strokes into 140 key strokes by tweeting...

> [5.209S, 145.806E] Arrived. Completed my row across the Pacific Ocean today. (@Vitiaz Strait near Madang)

... to announce to the world that she had become the first woman to row solo across the Pacific Ocean. The two year journey from San Francisco to Papua New Guinea included pauses in Hawaii and Kiribati (said kiri-bass) and was partly to raise awareness of the dangers of climate change and the quantities of plastics polluting the oceans.

The first person to row across the Pacific from America to Australia had also been English, one 36 year old Peter Bird in 1983. Determined also to be the first person to row the Pacific from West to East as well he disappeared in 1996 on his fifth attempt having met extreme weather not long after rowing out from Vladivostock in Russia.

Darwin's Point

The most distant part of Hawaii from Na'alehu is the snack-less Kure Atoll. It is 1566 miles to the north west of the Shaka Bar and Restaurant (page 103) and is the world's most northerly coral atoll.

At 28° 24' North its existence is significant. It was predicted to be there by Charles Darwin in 1842. He never saw or knew of Kure but reasoned that coral atolls could not exist any further north, the water temperature being too cold for suitable corals to flourish and grow upwards while the volcano beneath them was depressing the earth's crust and descending beneath the ocean surface. This latitude is called the Darwin Point. Beyond the Darwin Point the Hawaiian island chain continues all the way to Alaska but beneath the surface in the form of submerged seamounts and guyots (flat-topped sunken atolls).

The Darwin Point theory remained unproved for many years after his death. At least four 19th and early 20th century expeditions returned home having been unable to drill deep a deep enough hole to show that atolls are all perched on a, still sinking, volcano. But as a part of the US atomic bomb testing programme in the summer of 1951 at Enewatek Atoll, US Marshall Islands, two suitably deep holes were being drilled and just before 4,200 ft the core samples that had consistently been limestone were suddenly olivine basalt rock. Darwin had been proved right and the celebration the next year was literally the world's biggest bang—the detonation of Mike, the first 'hydrogen' bomb. Still the ninth biggest nuclear explosion ever, it was somewhat more powerful than anticipated and the whole of one of the islands comprising Enewatek Atoll no longer exists.

The surf breaking on the living coral forming a reef at Enewatek represents around 49 million years of upward growth from the coral exactly compensating for the downward sinking of the original volcano. Using a local human dimension as a ruler, the Enewatek volcano has been, and still is, descending by the width of your little fingernail every 350 years, 'every' being the crucial word when trying to comprehend the idea of time in matters geological. In 147 million years a canoe and paddle will be useful for the astrophysicists working at Hawaii's Astronomy Precint when it too will be another sandy coral atoll.

Douglas Adams

The Great Gig in Earl's Court

In January 1994 Douglas Adams joined a select group. He became a castaway on the BBC Radio 4 show *Desert Island Discs* (created 1942) in which a guest (there are 42 per year) chooses and talks about the eight records they would want on a hypothetical desert island which has a hypothetical record player. The host with Douglas Adams was Sue Lawley. Breaking with protocol he had posted his list of records on the interweb before the show for the benefit of fans in different countries wondering aloud about his forthcoming choice of music. Douglas Adams' desert island discs were, in order:

Man of Mystery—The Shadows
Drive My Car—The Beatles
Italian Concerto—JS Bach
B Minor Mass—JS Bach
Schubler Chorale Number 5—JS Bach
Requiem—Ligeti
Hearts and Bones—Paul Simon
All of Me—Ella Fitzgerald

The interweb message signed off with a joke: 'The list is

completely wrong, of course. I've been trying to choose my eight since I was about 10 years old, and in the end I just panicked.' Some of his favourites in contemporary music that didn't make it into the eight were: Procul Harum, Pink Floyd, Kate Bush, Elvis Costello, and Dire Straits. The Schubler Mass and the Italian Concerto were to be the first and last pieces of music played at his memorial service.

Between the music Douglas Adams spoke with excitement about computers and the interweb and that the Hitch-hiker's film was at last going to be made—it wasn't—and of feelings he believed were akin to being mildly manic-depressive, sometimes having massive amounts of energy and periods of not being able to think of ideas.

The program famously allows one luxury on the island, a choice guests have used in both prosaic and startling ways. Stephen Fry wanted a suicide pill, John Cleese asked for Michael Palin, and John Peel had a football. Douglas Adams requested a left-handed Martin D-28 guitar. Castaways also get to choose one book. Douglas Adams, comedy writer, chose a non-existent omnibus of all the golfing stories written by, comedy writer, PG Wodehouse. By the end of the year, behold and lo, BBC Radio 4 was broadcasting a series featuring tales from the most famous Wodehousian golfing character, The Oldest Member.

Pink Floyd got the opportunity to perform on stage with the talented Mr Adams on October 24th 1994 at the Earl's Court, London in a gig for his 42nd birthday. DNA played lead guitar on two tracks from *The Dark Side of the Moon*; *Brain Damage* and *Eclipse.*

Douglas Adams
Writer
1952 - 2001

Douglas Adams died trying to keep fit. The day was 11 May 2001. He was in a gym exercising with his trainer when he suffered a fatal heart attack. He had been in California working on the script in yet another bash at making the seemingly mythical Hitch-hiker's movie, and with his wife and young daughter was enjoying life in swanky Montecito on the warm south-slope gently carrying America down from the dry chaparral of the Santa Ynez Mountains into an infinity of Pacific Ocean. He liked living there. He was 49. His body was cremated in America and his ashes buried in London's Highgate Cemetery where a headstone stands. A memorial service held at St Martin's-in-the-Fields Church on London's Trafalgar Square was the first online broadcast from a place of worship. The distinction might have gained an interesting reaction. Douglas Adams differentiated strongly both between being agnostic ('silliness') and atheist, and between merely believing there isn't a God and being convinced. Parts of a bittersweet day, including funny memories and fine speeches from his friends, can still be seen and heard on the BBC website where it is, as I write, filed/hidden as 'cult' which may be a reference to St Martin's-in-the-Fields Church or Douglas Adams or both, but whatever the reason the simplest route to see and hear the poignant echoes of an exceptionally notable life is by using Google to search for 'Douglas Adams Memorial Service'.

Choosing the Right Parents

Polly Adams' dad was aged 42 on the day of her birth, he was Douglas Adams. Her mother is Jane Belson, who some three years earlier had married Douglas Adams.

In Nick Webb's official Douglas Adams biography *Wish You Were Here*, he describes the secular christening party held on Polly Adams' first birthday complete with non-godparents who in a mock contract agreed to be vicarious supreme being substitutes, and to perform a range of interesting duties including walking holidays in Iceland, long weekends in Venice and commiserating over the curmudgeonliness of the parents. Douglas Adams read Keats' sonnet *On First Looking Into Chapman's Homer*, a poem used to describe a major change in understanding, of seeing the whole picture.

DA In The DB

Christopher Adams was Douglas Adams' father and had a very remarkable car. After a painful divorce, Douglas Adams' father had remarried within three years to a wealthy widower from a Glasgow shipbuilding family whose husband had been killed in the war, and had two older daughters. She generously paid for Douglas and Sue Adams' education in fee-paying schools, Christopher Adams working as a probation officer. He was also a probation officer who drove an Aston Martin DB5. The DB5 was the Aston Martin of Aston Martins. It was the car driven by James Bond in the cinema. The teenage Douglas Adams had the experience of roaring around Europe in the ultimate head-turner. He can only have been the envy of any school-friend with even a remote interest in spies and cars.

Jane Belson, Douglas Adams' widow, allowed biographer Nick Webb access to his papers where he found Aston Martin magazines and pictures of the car with his father. And of course there is the DB which in the spy cipher of even a semi-competent agent means that when DA is 41 then DB is 42. For Christopher Adams, at least, an Aston Martin was close to being a part of the meaning of life. Douglas Adams also enjoyed interesting, exotic and powerful cars the list including a patriotic blue MG, Porsche 911, Porsche 928, VW Golf cabriolet, Lexus, and Mercedes 500. 'Like bringing a Ming vase to a football game' was Douglas Adams' assessment of driving a Porsche in London.

1, 2, ...42

On what would have been Douglas Adams' 51st birthday Professor Richard Dawkins, a friend who spoke at his memorial service, delivered the inaugural Douglas Adams Memorial Lecture on the subject of the strangeness of science. Douglas had written that one of his books about evolution, *The Blind Watchmaker*, had had a profound effect on his understanding of the science. Richard Dawkins was to aptly dedicate his book *The God Delusion* to Douglas Adams using one of his most loved quotations: '*Isn't it enough to see that a garden is beautiful without having to believe that there are fairies at the bottom of it too?*'

Professor Marcus du Sautoy, who succeeded Professor Dawkins as the Simonyi* Professor for the Public Understanding of Science, delivered the lecture in 2010. The subject was Forty two. His lecture described how Douglas Adams' Ultimate Answer really had recently become key to something long awaited by math buffs; the

---

* Mr Simonyi amassed a fortune working for Microsoft and has a Wikipedia biography that lists a single notable work: Microsoft Office. The next time a table in Microsoft Word extends itself unbidden five metres to the right of your screen and effects introductions with the desks and chairs next door, this is apparently the man to thank.

enabling of furthering understanding of the pattern of distribution of prime numbers as—drum roll here perhaps, then definitely followed by a big crash of cymbals—the very important third moment of the Riemann zeta function, it becoming part of one of the world's craziest sequences of numbers which—now—goes 1, 2, 42.

Python VII

Douglas Adams made a brief appearance in episodes 42 and 44 of the British legend, *Monty Python's Flying Circus*. He also wrote some of the fourth TV series, Douglas Adams and ex-Bonzo Dog Doo-Dah Band member, Neil Innes, being the only non-Pythons to receive writing credits.

With the Dalek-Botherers

Douglas Adams worked as a script editor and also wrote twelve episodes for the BBC TV series *Doctor Who*, which has, according to the BBC, appeared on television in 42 countries.

Douglas Adams refused to allow his scripts to be novelised for the regular small fee on account of his 'tendency to be a best-selling author'. The doctor during the time of Douglas Adams' work on the series was played by Tom Baker who held the role for the longest duration, seven years, using up no fewer than seven human 'companions' and a Timelady who was at a loose end. The dream-team pairing of having Douglas Adams do Dalek dialogues doesn't seem to have occurred to anyone.

Reverse Logic

Douglas Adams enjoyed telling people that he had been born in Cambridge with the initials DNA (middle name Noël) a year ahead of the discovery of the structure of the DNA molecule also in Cambridge. Arthur Dent in *The*

Hitch-hiker's Guide to The Galaxy, shares reversed initials with his creator and when he had to use a pseudonym writing for *Doctor Who* he chose David Agnew. A consideration in a search for the origin of 42 is that left-handed Douglas Adams was 24 when his idea for writing a radio series called *The Hitch-hiker's Guide to The Galaxy* was commissioned and could have reversed the digits.

The First UK Mac…

Douglas Adams is sometimes reported as having owned the first Apple Mac in the UK but this could well be apocryphal. Just five weeks before his death his friend Stephen Fry gave a humorous speech at a computer event in which he announced that he believed he had bought the third Apple Mac in the UK because 'Douglas Adams had bought the first two'. This was in part a joking reference to Douglas Adams' nature with regard to the acquisition of multiple instances of desirable gadgets; these included 24 left-handed guitars (a pleasing symmetry with 42 right-handers) with one stashed at the home of Ian Gilmour of Pink Floyd, a fine selection of expensive cameras and lenses, no shortage of mobile phones and more computers than their owner claimed to be able to count.

The Best Selling Humorous Book...On This Planet

Exactly how many Douglas Adams books have been sold seems impossible to know. A figure not un-adjacent to 20,000,000 might be in the zone. The original guide is listed by one source as being the 37th best-selling adult fiction written in English but significantly *The Hitch-hiker's Guide to The Galaxy* is almost certainly the world's best selling humorous book written for adults.

The Forty two card was played to promote a number of editions. A 25th anniversary edition included 42 pages of Douglas Adams related material with 21 writers adding 42 words each about memories of first the guide. The price of the collected works in the United States was $42 and the ISBN number of the US illustrated edition ended with 42.

A is for Americana

The Forty-Second Floor

The first building to have a lift to the forty-second floor was New York's Singer Building. It was also the first building with a forty-second floor. Built in 1908 by the sewing machine company of the same name it was the first skyscraper to be taller than both the Great Pyramid and the cathedrals of Europe. A posthumous fifth record also belongs to the ex-Singer: it was the world's tallest peacefully deconstructed building, being succeeded in 1968 by a roomier structure on its former site which was alongside the World Trade Centre's Twin Towers.

Isaac Merritt Singer the company founder had died thirty-two years earlier but is more than notable for his industrial capacity for simultaneously aggregating families. Having perfected the low-priced sewing machine, and its marketing, Singer became very wealthy, very quickly. Resembling in appearance the well-upholstered English king, Edward VII, Isaac Singer was living in considerable comfort with his second wife and family on New York's Fifth Avenue until a day in the early 1860s when his wife saw him out driving in a carriage with the mother of one of his three other contemporaneous families. His domestic world went spinning; his legitimate wife had him arrested for bigamy, and in disgrace he went to Europe with another 'wife' and five children. In Paris this relationship ended when he became well acquainted with Isabella, who then became his third legal wife.

He took Isabella to England when war threatened Paris and wanting a single home large enough for all of his children he set about building a one hundred room mansion, as one did, near the sea in rural Devon and which he called 'The Wigwam'. He died in 1875 shortly before the building was completed. His will left fourteen million dollars (comparable with $1.2 billion in 2011) and acknowledged 22 children. Isabella Singer took the children back to Paris where she married a Dutch violinist who utilised his wife's fortune, amongst other things, to collect superior tools of his trade including Strads (around ten) and Guarneris (several). For a wedding present (according to Indiana's *Crawfordsville Weekly Argus*) Isabella paid $10,000 to buy her new husband the Italian title of Duke of Camposelice, with Isabella styling herself the Duchess of Camposelice under the buy-one-and-receive-one-gratis rule. The marriage was unhappy, and short, and then he died. Isabella Singer remarried (to a second violinist) and was then to provide the Singer name with a further and positively un-improveable connection with New York by becoming it is believed, the sculptor Frédéric Bartholdi's model for the Statue of Liberty whose statistics—in case anyone is considering I may be drifting from the plot—include a very healthy forty two feet of right arm.

In The Dawn's Early Light

On 9/11 the fourth target had either been the White House or the Capitol Building. The heroism of the people on Flight 93 saved Washington from murder and destruction. Few people know that the devastation intended for the fabric of the nation's capital would have been a repetition of a successful attack by a 42-year-old Englishman. The first attack on Washington happened during the 'Second War of Independence' or War of 1812 against Britain, which had been failing to respect American sovereignty.

In the summer of 1814 British troops commanded by Rear Admiral Sir George Cockburn had entered

Washington and torched the White House, the Library of Congress, the Capitol Building and the Treasury Building before raising the British flag over the American capital. The destruction galvanised the American forces and resulted in a second flag being raised—now immortalised in song and probably the most famous flag in the world.

The Great Garrison Flag at Fort McHenry on the entrance to Baltimore harbour was then the largest battle flag ever flown. An early example of the American confidence that best is biggest, the garrison commander, one George Armistead, had commissioned the flag to signal America's hold of a key defensive position to any approaching British. Costing $405.90 with dimensions of 42ft by 30ft the 15 Stars and 15 Stripes were stitched together in 42 days from 400 yards of cloth by Mary Young Pickersgill, her daughter, two nieces, and a servant.

After the burning of Washington the British sailed further into Chesapeake Bay planning to capture Baltimore. They landed a few miles from Fort McHenry on the 12th September but quickly lost their commanding general who was one of the 42 British killed at the battle of North

Point. The advance was halted while Fort McHenry was bombarded by naval cannons and rockets to remove the defensive lynchpin.

Under a flag of truce on a British ship were three Americans. One was Francis Scott Key who had been parlaying for the release of a captured friend. He had feared that Fort McHenry would not withstand the British assault but to demonstrate their apparent invulnerability, overnight Major Armistead had raised his Giant Garrison Flag in the place of a regular-sized version. The words of the *Star Spangled Banner* are Francis Scott Key's on seeing that the Stars and Stripes still flew over the fort, and America:

> *O! say does that star-spangled banner yet wave,*
> *O'er the land of the free and the home of the brave?*

The attack had failed and the British were to shortly sign a peace treaty declaring the war over. The giant flag—slightly foreshortened by early souvenir hunters—is now displayed in the Smithsonian, close to where Cockburn had dared to fly a British flag over the home of the brave.

B Minus

A smaller facsimile of the historic Star Spangled Banner still flies over Fort McHenry and shows the unusual 15 stars and 15 stripes that represented the fifteen states of the 1814 union. It is unique in being the only US flag, either previously or since, with 15 rather than 13 stripes. Each time a new state had joined the union a new flag was required. The most recent occasion was in 1960, when Hawaii joined, and the designer was a 16 year old Ohio junior school student, Bob Heft who had been born in 1942 in Saginaw, Michigan. He chose the idea of designing a new flag in a school project and made a prototype fifty star design using the forty-eight star family flag. His teacher was under-impressed and awarded Bob's flag a B minus. This was retrospectively upgraded to an A after President Eisenhower had agreed that the new design could shortly be viewed flying everywhere across America and around the world.

Yours very truly (Leó Szilárd)

In 1933 the Nazis under Adolf Hitler passed a law banning Jews from teaching at universities, or holding any position of authority. Einstein*, although now a Swiss citizen, was listed as an enemy of the Nazi regime with a bounty of $5000 on his life, so like many other German scientists Einstein fled to the United States, arriving in 1935. Just before the start of WW II in 1938 the atom was first knowingly split in Germany, being discovered by Lise Meitner who had fled from Germany to Sweden but had continued working with Otto Hahn and Fritz Straßman who had stayed in Berlin (Only Hahn was to receive a Nobel Prize for the achievement).

The Nazi War Ministry had been informed in April 1939 that there might be the potential for a nuclear weapon and work began. Aware of developments Einstein signed a letter in August 1939 to President Roosevelt warning that Nazi Germany might develop an atomic bomb and that the United States should therefore consider also investigating nuclear weapons.

The writer was not Einstein but a 42 year old Hungarian,

---

* Einstein and religion was a major subject of interest during his lifetime; he was brought up in a non-observant Jewish family and first attended a Catholic school but did not believe in anthropomorphic concepts of God, saying he had a deeply religious attitude… if that attitude comprised knowing that mankind was unable to understand all the beauty and complexity of the universe. He was a Humanist.

Leó Szilárd, who was also a Jew and had also escaped from the Nazis. Together with Enrico Fermi he had already enterprisingly patented the nuclear reactor. Just before the start of WW II while working in New York Szilárd and Fermi made the discovery that nuclear weapons could almost certainly be manufactured.

It took the United States and her allied workers six years and an intensive programme to successfully test the first nuclear bomb. The German programme did not get close to producing a bomb. In 1942 the German effort was scaled back on the grounds of not being likely to help win the war while at the same time in the US the Manhattan Project had conducted the first controlled nuclear reaction in the world.

Tellingly for what-if alternatives to the history of the world a key to the very different outcomes of the two programmes was a single discovery made by one man—who might have been working on the German bomb if the Nazis hadn't been anti-Semitic. An impurity, boron, had been stopping supposedly pure carbon from working properly in the production of explosive bomb material. The Germans had to use a big work-around that needed heavy water as an alternative to the much simpler carbon. Making heavy water in turn needed a massive amount of energy and could only quickly be done in a single requisitioned plant in Norway where production was successfully sabotaged (as shown in the 1965 film *The Heroes of Telemark*).

The person responsible for solving the boron problem for the United States rather than Germany was Leó Szilárd who had, of course, drafted the famous Einstein letter to Roosevelt that began the whole US nuclear programme.

Looking for America

'Larry, what say we stop and eat?' said Sergey. The Google Street View Camera Car had been following the 42 into the Appalachians and the guys had worked up a serious appetite. They pulled up and, sighing ever-so-slightly, Sergey muted *Bohemian Rhapsody* and, for what seemed like the millionth time, reminded Larry to press the camera's Big Red Stop Button.

Standing on the corner in Centralia, Pennsylvania they took in the scene on Locust Avenue. It was foggy and it was raining but Sergey immediately identified a problem. Centralia was short of things. Most importantly somewhere two hungry Google guys could refuel before continuing on the great road trip to film all of America. No Arby's. No McDonald's. No Wendys. No Taco Bell. Nada. Getting back in the car and slowing only momentarily as Sergey waited for Larry to remember to press the camera's Big Green Go Button, they set off to look for the rest of America.

Tracking over to Centralia, PA in Google Earth confirms Larry and Sergey's story. It is a fall day in 2009 and it is foggy and it is raining. Traffic is running with its lights on.

Shuffle around and you see roads connecting lots aplenty with almost none bearing any sign of a house. Nor are there any stores, garages, or oases for seekers of good food, for Centralia is almost a ghost town, created by an underground coal fire started in 1962 and causing the relocation of eleven hundred people and their supporting businesses at a cost of $42 million in 1984.

Two facts I found moderately alarming when reading about Centralia are a) that underground coal fires are natural, some coals can spontaneously combust in thin air at a midge's over blood heat, and b) that there are many thousands of coal fires all round the world combining to puff out CO_2 on an epic scale. The pioneering Lewis and Clark saw coal burning in Wyoming in 1804. Germany has a Burning Mountain near Dudweiler that has been aflame since 1688. Australia has another Burning Mountain which is the world's oldest, alight for 6000 years. In North Dakota there is a Burning Coal Vein Campground for the vacationer interested in conflagration. An international body is dedicated to sharing information on ways of eliminating and controlling underground coal fires.

Centralia's double misfortune was first to have a fire that

was self-inflicted (burning the garbage in a badly chosen landfill site that comprised unsealed coal workings had started the whole thing off), and then for that fire to spread with alacrity through old coal workings right beneath the town. But despite the 1984 relocation opportunity some residents chose to stay. At first patient, by 1992 the state of Pennsylvania declared 'eminent domain' which changed the status of the remaining residents into squatters in their own homes. In 2002 the postal zipcode was taken away—though slotting 17927 into one online property tracker indicates that 3-bed homes in Centralia are commanding prices of over $145,000.

In the summer of 2010 nine Centralians remained in five houses, all under official orders to quit that had been received a while ago. Poignantly they maintain memories and links with family and friends from former, happier times by keeping their cemeteries in immaculate condition. And there is a new phenomenon, a growing stream of visitors. In summer there are enough to consider opening a burger franchise.

The Elevator Pitch

Working or living in taller and taller buildings never caught on until the invention of the safety lift. Elisha Otis began his Otis Elevator Company in New York when he was forty two. The first customer was a Benjamin Newhouse who had lost two employees to a fatal lift accident and in 1853 purchased an Otis Life-Saving Steam Elevator to lift materials in his furniture factory. The world's first safety lift was built without the aid of drawings, blueprints or prototypes; Elisha Otis just made it. Business was slow at first but Elisha Otis had the cure. At the first world fair in New York in 1854 he would be lifted above the spectators in a demonstration model before asking a colleague to axe the rope. The regularly repeated demonstration—its safety mechanism always worked—drew attentive crowds, stimulated sales, and was a big draw for the Exposition.

The first Otis passenger safety lift remains and is in working condition. It can be located at 488 Broadway, New York, behind the notable cast-iron façade of the E.V. Haughwout Building. This had been the premises for a popular store selling finest cut glass, china and porcelain goods. Customer footfall increased considerably when the novelty of a ride in a lift was added to the store's proposition, even though the hydraulic mechanism took 64 seconds to lift the curious around 42 feet to the top floor.

Of a sudden safety lifts literally turned city property values upside down. The highest apartments and hotel rooms had traditionally had the lowest rents and rates just because of all the tiresome stairs. With a lift these became the most desirable because of the views and the pleasing separation from the noise and dust of the street. Before Elisha Otis a hotel penthouse had been somewhere interested guests might venture to admire the view from the janitor's billet. Otis lifts are used by the Tower (Burj) Khalifa, the world's tallest structure. The observation lifts are the fastest in the world carrying 42 people at 42 feet per 0.7 seconds—ninety times faster than the E.V. Haughwout building's passenger lift #0000001.

Junior President

The youngest President of the United States was 42, VP Theodore Roosevelt (third from the left on Mt Rushmore) becoming the 26th President on September 14th 1901 following the assassination of the 25th President, William McKinley. McKinley was the third President to be assassinated. He was shot by a 28-year-old anarchist Leon Czolgosz at the Pan-American exposition in Buffalo, New York State. His killer refused to speak with defence lawyers and was electrocuted on the 42nd day after the death of the President (who had lived for several days after the shooting). A stone, now within a suburban housing estate, marks the place where the assassination occurred, 65 miles north of the 42nd parallel.

Theodore Roosevelt was quickly a popular and famous President. 'Speak softly and carry a big stick' he famously said and became the first American to win a Nobel prize, winning the 1906 Peace Prize for mediating the end of Russian-Japanese war. At 47 he was a year younger than Barack Obama was in 2009 when he also won the Peace Prize. TR did not accept the money, believing that it belonged to the office he held rather than himself.

His second son, Kermit Roosevelt, was named after his mother and her brother who had died as an infant. The name has clicked so well with succeeding Roosevelt generations that it possesses its own Wikipedia disambiguation page to helpfully disambiguate between the original Kermit, Kermit Jr, Kermit Jr (II), and Kermit III, who is a law professor and writer.

Channel 42

When staying at the scenically matchless Stanley Hotel in Colorado be sure to remember to dial 42 on the TV remote. Channel 42 shows Stanley Kubrick's 1980 horror film *The Shining* on a continuous loop. Stephen King stayed at The Stanley Hotel in Colorado prior to writing *The Shining*. The Overlook in the film where Jack Nicholson's character is the winter caretaker was based on the Stanley Hotel.

The Stanley Hotel was built by one of the two brothers of Stanley Steamers fame. Steam-powered, Stanleys were the fastest cars in the world from 1906 to 1911, racing about at 28 mph. They were soon to be superseded by much cheaper, mass-produced, petrol-engined cars such as Ford's Model T.

Notables

QE42

The Queen of the United Kingdom, Elizabeth II, was the 42nd most powerful woman in the world in 2009 according to Forbes magazine. This was great news for Britain's oldest reigning monarch, having risen 16 places from 58th in 2008. Ahead of her Majesty in 2009 were Oprah Winfrey (41st), Michelle Obama (40th) and Marina Berlusconi (33rd).

Number one as the world's most powerful woman was the German Chancellor Angela Merkel according to the Forbes' people who assess the power of all the world's women but who have not had the pleasure of spending quality time arm-wrestling with Mrs Gill.

Lot 33

In 2008, in a sale catalogue for Christie's London auction-rooms, lot 33 was described as a boomerang that had belonged to Captain Cook's widow, Elizabeth. Disappointingly it was withdrawn when its provenance was questioned, one Australian had declaimed that the treasure was no more than a 'bent stick'. This original radio transcript has now been made up to provide the clarification needed to satisfy the most demanding of boomerang buyers.

Dramatis Personæ	(A Vogon stagehand. Seen shifting a stage direction into the wings as the curtains open)
James T. Cook	(An easy on the ear, Clive James sound-clone)
Elizabeth Cook	(Anne Stallybrass, or if not available, Jane Austen)

It is 1771 and the scene is a small house in the East End of London, unfashionably close to the docks. Thirtysomething Elizabeth Cook keels a blackened pot. [F/X: Footsteps outside,

and cheerful whistling.] A jaunty nautical type nears carrying a tune. Waltzing Matilda. The door opens and forty-two year old Lieutenant James T. Cook of the British Navy stands in the doorway, beaming from a tanned face.

JAMES Hi honey, I'm home!

ELIZABETH ...James!

James drops an armload of parcels. They embrace with a view to sex later.

ELIZABETH ...where have you been! You just said your new fo'c'sle was here and you were disappearing down the Lord Lucan to enquire if anyone was desirous of availing themselves of a bit of a jolly round the estuary, and...then...nothing...

JAMES I know - I know - I know - but the sun was shining, the sky was blue, and there was an ace blow on. The boys were enjoying themselves and we thought we'd kind of keep going, for a bit.

ELIZABETH That was three years ago hen-wit. *Three years*. Where the Belgium have you been for *three years*? Supper's ruined.

JAMES (**checking off list on fingers**) The Society Islands, The Friendly Islands, The Navigator Islands, Easter Island, The Eponymous Cook Islands, New Zealand, Norfolk Island and then, bang, we hit Australia. Look darling, engravings of the collision for the insurance fellas. Here, open the presents.

ELIZABETH (**unwrapping a half-full (Oz adaption), or half-empty (Pom adaption), bottle of Bundaberg Rum**). What, is, Bundaberg?

JAMES Our first great Australian discovery, that's what; the old *Endeavour* was being completely chewed to pieces by Teredo worms when spunky little Kylie at the Kurnell Bottle-o suggested buying some Bundy to treat the ship's timbers. Plus, she said, every hogshead's rammed full of vitamin C which we'd surely be needing if the Cointreau went low on the way home; and there was a special offer on for us platinum loyalty card customers.

ELIZABETH ...and...this...thing?

JAMES My dearest, you are holding the first euphemism from down-under ever to reach the shores of England.

ELIZABETH Sir. Though book-learning I may lack, 'tis well I know the difference between a penis and your didgeridoo, I think.

JAMES Fair enough, how about first wang with the boomerang…

ELIZABETH James, need'st I remind thee, ensconced we are in the East End of London. The second biggest city in the world. What good be a boomerang? Emu is very, very, extremely scarce. Who hereabouts has seen Drop-bear spoor? There are a complete lack of Wallaby and Kangaroo...

THE VOICE Lieutenant James T. Cook RN frowns. He looks at his new K1 Larcum Kendall; at £450 it is the most expensive chronometer in the world and the big hand is on ten. A face considered dour, even in its native Yorkshire, smiles.

JAMES Elizabeth. Eyes on me. Relax. The boys will still be in the Lord Lucan: we can sail on the morrow's arvo tide. No worries Liz – we'll fetch you some 'roo.

FADE

Mosi Oa Tunya?

The Victoria Falls were named for Queen Victoria in 1855 by explorer David Livingstone when he was forty-two and at the height of his discovering powers. His name is their second name, the falls already being known more lyrically as *Mosi oa Tunya* meaning Thundering Smoke. Heights, water volumes, and breadths of waterfalls are contested as different ways of claiming waterfall bragging rights, and the Victoria Falls heads the category for being the biggest sheet of falling water in the world.

Livingstone didn't undersell his discovery, writing that their beauty was greater than anything you could discern in England and that 'scenes so lovely must have been gazed upon by angels in their flight.' It was not disclosed whether any hospitality had been received from the tourist board. The falls have two statues of Livingstone; one for the Zimbabwean side and one for the Zambian.

Livingstone died eighteen years later, very ill but still bent on exploring and trying to locate the source of the River Nile. After his death Dr Livingstone was sub-divided; his heart being buried in Africa near Chief Chitambo's village in Zambia, the balance of his remains being in London's Westminster Abbey. At a remote spot towards the north of Tanganyika Lake there is The Livingstone Stone where—or near where—the even more remarkable Sir Henry Stanley located Livingstone and may—or may not—have said, 'Dr Livingstone, I presume.'

Dave the Wise

1936 was a whirlwind of a year for the new king of England. In a single period of 366 days King Edward VIII became the first King Dave (David to family and friends) of the United Kingdom and the Dominions, and the first monarch to fly as well as rule over England. There was also the serious matter of finding a birthday cake large enough for the 42 candles that would wow Wallis on his first birthday as King. This box ticked he wasted not a Royal moment before mastering the demanding skillset required to precipitate an abdication crisis, while at the same time—the man knew about multi-tasking—sensibly synchronising royal diaries with the rest of the world by administering a royal knock on the head to the *fin de siècle* wackiness known as Sandringham Time.

Sandringham Time

The notion of Sandringham Time (ST) was created by Edward VIII's grandfather, Edward VII (think cigars, lots of cigars), as an adroit means of creating more daylight for hunting and shooting during the winter. All the clocks around Sandringham, their Norfolk palace in the country, were set 30 minutes ahead of GMT and the rest of the realm except—to avoid the possibility of palace lag—the clocks in Balmoral and Windsor Castles, which were also set to ST.

After Edward's abdication his brother, George VI, had to put in an offer to his ex-king to buy back Sandringham House and Balmoral Castle because both properties were privately owned by the King rather than going with the job of being monarch in the manner of, say, a Buckingham Palace or a Windsor Castle. The purchase prices were secret but are likely to have been, at the very least, several multiples of £42.

Eddie Izzard

Followed by an ice-cream van playing the theme from *Chariots of Fire* and giving away ice-cream, comedian Eddie Izzard ran through St Albans on the penultimate marathon of the 43 he completed within 51 days during 2009 to raise money for the charity Sports Relief.

Zero Pound PM

Britons using Australia's assisted migration scheme were known as ten pound poms—ten pounds being all you needed to pay for a voyage of 42 days (depending on ship and any stops) from England to Australia via the Suez Canal. The scheme ran from the 1940s until 1973 when the price increased to £75. Some of the well-known ten pound poms include:

Name	**Sailed**	**Age**	**Achievement**
Harold Larwood	1950	45	Cricket fast bowler in the 1932 'fix Bradman' bodyline series
Carol Jones (Minogue)	1955	12	Mum of Kylie (42) and Danii Minogue
Frank Tyson	1960	30	Cricketing bowler 'Typhoon Tyson'
Mick Hadley	1962	19	Lead vocalist with rock group 'The Purple Hearts' featuring Lobby Loyde
Robert Wood	1963	c. 13	NSW Senator for Nuclear Disarmament Party. Disqualified in 1988 when revealed he was not a citizen of Oz
David Stratton	1963	22	Popular TV and newspaper film critic

Name	Sailed	Age	Achievement
Richard Pengelley	1966	5	Water Polo Olympian '82 and '86
Julia Gillard	1966	4	The current Australian Prime Minister. Born in Wales, parents made no extra payment to bring children
Peter Allen	c.1966	c. 20	UK Presenter, BBC Radio Five Live. About three-in-four assisted migrants made Australia their new home
Chris & Grace Jackman	1967	-	Parents of film star Hugh Jackman (42)
John Hamblin	c.1968	c. 33	'Funny John', Australian children's TV *Play School* presenter. Appeared in *The Prisoner* (1967) and *Riptide* (1969)
John Young	1970s	c. 24	Joined the Australian 'Rich List' after establishing the Great Southern Group. Left the list in 2009 when the GSG went into liquidation

People from many other countries have migrated and continue to migrate to Australia. Over 42% of Australians were born elsewhere.

Super Hero

'And I didn't get killed in the flat'. Test pilot Chuck Yeager's unique turn of phrase describing the last portion of a unique escape from death. On somewhere around his 42nd flight in a rocket version of the Lockheed Starfighter he was 21 miles up to test the plane's performance limits, which he found when it started spinning uncontrollably. After being dropped nearly 20 miles he availed himself of 'the egress system' to become the first pilot to eject in an oxygenated pressure suit. Then, as seen in the 1983 film *The Right Stuff* made twenty years later and in which Yeager makes a cameo appearance as a bartender, there was a situation-shift: moving from bad into downright disastrous. After ejection, the pilot needs to be ejected in turn from his ejector seat by the 'butt-kicker'. This worked, but his falling ejector seat stayed too close and snagged with his own chute. The heavy seat crashed into him and a rocket with un-burnt fuel smashed through his visor, injuring his face, and burning in the oxygen 'like a blow-torch'. This resulted in very serious burns to his face and neck. Then he made the ground—landing softly enough to escape being 'killed in the flat'.

Between Edwards Air Force Base where Yeager flew and Los Angeles is Air Force Plant 42 the manufacturing facility for secret military aircraft. The area includes the Lockheed Skunkworks, famed for quick project development, the first being completion in 143 days of the first US jet fighter during WWII. This was later followed by the U2 and Blackbird spy planes, the F117 Nighthawk, and the F22 Raptor. The B-2 Stealth bomber and the space shuttles were assembled at Plant 42.

Now hanging in the Smithsonian Museum, as if in perpetual flight, is the bright orange 'Glamorous Glennis'. This is the Bell-X1 rocket plane in which Chuck Yeager, named after his wife, was first to be confirmed to have broken the sound barrier—which he recorded as having occurred at an altitude of 42,000 feet. This was a top secret at the time in 1947 as the question of what would happen to a plane and pilot on breaking the sound barrier (Mach 1 = 700 mph at that height) had been the subject of serious theorising. 'Grandma could be up there sipping lemonade.' Chuck Yeager later said. Now a grandfather and a retired Major General, at the age of 86 he broke the sound barrier again in 2009 flying an F16—making him the world's fastest octogenarian.

Supper with Louisa and Francis

Wondering what to talk about was never a concern for friends invited round for a spot of supper with Louisa and Francis Galton at 42 Rutland Gate in London's well-heeled South Kensington. Their host was possibly able to deploy the widest range of interesting dinner party conversations ever known.

Nervous and wanting to make a cautious start? Try the conversational slow ball of weather. You would immediately know the the correct door had been knocked. Francis Galton was first person ever to draw a weather map, with his first efforts appearing in *The Times* newspaper of London and running ever since.

How about a round of holiday one-upmanship? Ever polite Francis, if asked, could match anyone. In 1839 as an adventuresome 17 year old he travelled alone to Constantinople (Istanbul) followed by a gap year thing travelling up the Nile. His appetite for foreign food whetted he then undertook serious exploration being the first European to reach remotest Ovamboland—in the area of Namibia and Angola of today.

Thinking of writing a book? Francis could probably help. After his African adventures he became a celebrity author by writing a book called *Art of Travel*—still in print. Akin to Ray Mears and Bear Grylls as Victorians fancying something different, the first page squishes silly fears of possible death by coolly observing that natives rarely murder newcomers. Everything else you might need to know included the knack of lighting a pipe in a hurricane (do it under your horse); keeping your clothes dry in a downpour (take them off, fold them up, and sit on them); and in case the indigenes hadn't read the bit about newcomers, how to sleep with your gun (stock between head and arm, barrel between legs).

A divertissement while the soup course is cleared? Ask about his interest in a medical career. Francis felt that to best understand the various drugs and medicines he would try them all, in alphabetical order. Surviving through A and B, he was most parts of the way through C when he picked up a bottle of Croton Oil. This afflicted him with such an episode of diarrhoea that further drug experimentation was placed on permanent hold. (The extreme efficacy of Croton Oil can be gauged when it is learned that the US Navy added it to pure alcohol torpedo fuel to keep sailors from drinking it during WW II). And there was also the interesting day in Ovamboland when, purely for scientific interest of course, he utilised his sextant to measure the vital statistics of a Khoikhoi lady without needing to make her acquaintance.

Any gossip? This was an immediate conversation-starter as Francis Galton was the ultimate people person. Having been originally stimulated by the great debate about evolution created by Darwin—who being a half-cousin to Galton could conceivably have been facing you over the carrots—he measured everything measurable about thousands of people; eyesight, stride, reactions, fingerprints, weight, height and more. By-products of this effort were his invention of fingerprinting for forensic purposes and new ideas now known as statistics (James Surowiecki's excellent book *The Wisdom of Crowds* opens with the story of Francis Galton's calculation that the average of all the entries in a guess-the-weight-of-the-ox competition was almost exactly the beast's true heft).

Sex, religion, or politics? Emboldened by the wine, you might fancy some controversy with the trifle. Francis Galton had undertaken infinitesimally detailed study into the family relationships amongst groups of high-achievers in areas of achievement as different as English High Court judges (205 years' worth) and north-country wrestlers and even poets. Nature not nurture was the stronger he wrote in *Hereditary Genius*, developing the idea of eugenics or the self-direction of human evolution as a smart means of speeding Darwin's far-too-slow natural selection. He also suggested, years ahead of other observers that the world's population should be deliberately controlled to match the resources of the planet.

Measuring the success of a dinner party? After the 'good-nights' and clip-clopping of horses away from Rutland Gate the evening may not have quite been over for the brain of Francis Galton (he became Sir Francis just before his death). There is an account that he had a means of measuring the pressure applied under the legs of the chairs around his dining-table, as he had a theory that people who were mutually attracted tended to lean towards each other, from which data he was able to keep a score on just who had been getting along a little too well with whom that evening.

Checking Out and Leaving

Some notable people and one other primate who died in their 43rd Year.

Name	Year	Cause of Death	Notability
Sir Anthony Van Dyck, Artist	1641	Fell ill when seeking work in Paris	Painted Charles I (beheaded later) with a distinctive facial hair assembly later called a Vandyck. Yet another famous Belgium
Madame de Pompadour	1764	Tuberculosis	Official chief mistress of Louis XV of France, trysting apartments can be seen in the Palace of Versailles
Prince Albert, Husband of Queen Victoria	1861	Possible typhoid	The mildly imposing 176ft Albert Memorial in central London was personally commissioned by Queen Victoria
Modest Mussorgsky, Russian composer	1881	Alcoholism	His *Night on a Bare Mountain* was used by Disney in *Fantasia* but was not performed in his lifetime.
R J Mitchell, British Spitfire designer	1937	Rectal cancer	Only ever saw prototypes of his famous Spitfire fighter flying

Name	Year	Cause of Death	Notability
Robert Kennedy, former Attorney General, New York Senator, and Presidential Candidate	1968	Murdered while campaigning after winning the key California primary	His killer, Sirhan Sirhan, is 67 and serving a life sentence
Elvis Presley	1977	Autopsy first stated uneven heart rhythm	Re-opened to re-conclude heart attack probably associated with polypharmacy, or 'too many drugs'
Peter Tosh, Reggae star	1987	Murdered for money	Original Wailer, with Bob Marley on *Catch a Fire* and *Burnin'*. And a talented unicyclist
Jacqueline du Pré	1987	Multiple sclerosis	British cellist of legendary talent. Career of only 11 years. Yo-Yo Ma has one of her two Strads
Washoe	2007	Natural causes. i.e. no monkey business	Washoe was the name of the chimpanzee first able to use sign language to interact with the humans at Washington University
Gary Coleman	2010	Fell and hit head	Famous child star in the role of Arnold Jackson in *Diff'rent Strokes*.

Health, Foods and Diets

Death of an Acronym

Tucked inside the back cover of my reserve copy of *The Nitpicker's Guide for Classic Trekkers* there is a carefully folded sheet of paper. On it is my list of the 42 most famous Belgians, where at the foot of the list is Baudoin, who died in 1993 having been King of the Belgians for 42 years.

At number 41 is Adolpe Quételet (1796-1874) a very clever Belgian indeed, succeeding notably in multiple areas of scientific discovery. In the mid 19th century he introduced QI to the world. The Quételet Index (QI) neatly expresses the relationship between your weight and your height. This was so until 1972 when the more aggressive American three-letter-acronym (TLA) set about supplanting the shyer European two-letter-acronym (TLA). The QI very quickly lost territory to the Body Mass Index (BMI) and even though it was the exact, same and identical (ESI) calculation, within a very few years for all practical purposes the poor QI was quite inert.

QI

A royal prerogative of the King of Rock and Roll seems to have been the right to suppress the release of both the weight and height data needed to calculate Elvis Presley's QI, and later BMI, but they may have reached 42. His weight had once been said to be 19 stone, without corroboration this means nothing but, if so, at an average height of 5 foot 10 inches his figure would have been 38. At 21 stone it would have reached 42. A QI of over 40 is classed as morbidly obese and in 2000 4.2 million Americans were estimated to be morbidly obese—bulging to 15 million in 2009. In the Elvis country of Tennessee 68% of adults were officially classified as overweight in 2007, one of the three worst states in America for obesity.

Celebrity	QI or BMI
Mr Simpson	32 ~ 43
Elvis Presley	38 ~ 42 ~ ?
Statue of Liberty	96
Michelangelo's David	227

V42

Queen Victoria had 42 grandchildren. The last one standing was Princess Alice, Countess of Athlone who died in 1981 at the age of 97. Despite apparently good health Princess Alice carried type B haemophilia, as did her grandmother (Queen Victoria), her father, and at least six of the other grandchildren. Type B was first called Royal Disease because it so affected the British Royal Family, later being clinically known as Christmas Disease after a young sufferer, Stephen Christmas, who was one of the first to be involved in the study of the condition.

Only boys and men suffer the bleeding, and it is now believed that the gene mutation causing the quite rare disease (1 in 25,000 births) keeps re-occurring spontaneously during sperm production. Victoria's father was Prince Edward, Duke of Kent, the fourth son of George III who was 51 when Victoria was conceived (dying before his new daughter's first birthday). He had remained single until the death of the King's only legitimate grandchild in 1818 when he and the other unmarried sons raced to both marry and produce an heir, a race he won with the birth of Princess Alexandrina Victoria. His age at the time may have increased the likelihood of the haemophilia mutation occurring.

Princess Alice's father, who was a sufferer, had a physician in permanent attendance but died aged 30 after a fall at the yacht club in Cannes. Princess Alice had two sons and a daughter. The younger son, Maurice, died before his first birthday. The older son, Rupert, Viscount Trematon, died of bleeding following a car crash in France in 1928 at the age of 20 while still a student at Cambridge. The mutated gene transmitted to four other royal families and most notably Tsarevitch Alexei, the only son of Tsar Nicholas of Russia, who was murdered by the Bolsheviks at the age of 13. The last of Victoria's descendants to die of haemophilia was Infante Gonzalo the fourth surviving son of King Alfonso X of Spain, who died in Austria in 1934 after a minor car accident when he was 19, appearing to bring to an end the transmission of a miserable chance mutation that had happened 116 years before.

The Spheniscidaean Diet

History is mixed as to whether John Davis was 42 or 35 (so we'll go with the first one) when he became the first

European to land on the Falkland Islands. An outstanding expert in ocean navigation, he was not so good with food. On the Falklands his men grazed extensively from the island's copious supply of Gentoo and Rockhopper penguins, and before sailing home to England Davis had the idea of provisioning the *Desire* with 14,000 cured penguins.

His logical reasoning was that by feeding a sailor a penguin a day the Spheniscidaean diet would stop the very much feared onset of the pestilential scurvy that occurred on ocean voyages. Raw penguin does indeed possess sufficient Vitamin C to do the job, so it should have worked, but fatally the carcases of the stored birds rotted because of ineffective curing. The cost was the death of most of his men (sixty-two of the seventy-six) before 14 survivors managed to beach the ship on the coast of Ireland.

In the Falkland Islands, John Davis is remembered every 14th August when Falklands Day is celebrated on the day he discovered the islands. As a mark of respect, none of the bars or restaurants serve any penguin dishes.

The Hitler Diet

Shortly before he became leader of Nazi Germany, Adolf Hitler turned vegetarian in 1931 at the age of 42, until his death either never or rarely eating meat (exactly which is un-discernible as accounts conflict).

The decision appears to have been made after the death of Geli Raubal, his half-sister's 23-year-old daughter with whom he was believed to be having a sexual relationship. Geli's body was discovered in her Uncle Alf's smart Munich flat with one bullet wound—inflicted by Hitler's own gun. A letter she had been writing to a friend allegedly detailed future plans and ended in mid-sentence, yet the 'suicide' was not closely investigated. One of the detectives had been Heinrich Müller who later became the head of Hitler's new Gestapo. After the defeat of the Nazis, Müller was the most senior Nazi to evade capture and possibly successfully disappear.

The David Blaine Diet

On 17th October 2003 in London, David Blaine had been suspended in a perspex box over the Thames for 42 days.

Emerging on schedule two days later he had survived without food drinking only water and losing 54 pounds in weight. The estimated rate of calorie loss had been 4725 calories a day. By not eating, and drinking only water and staying in a box, he averaged a loss of 8 pounds and 9 ounces each week.

Southern Cooking

Close to the southernmost part of Big Island, Hawaii is Na'alehu the southernmost town in the United States. Hawaii is the forty-second most populous state.

The Shaka Bar and Restaurant is the only bar in Na'alehu so you should take some care not to miss it. Having found it, don't wait for valet-parking, there is none. Do belly up to the bar and order the coconut shrimp with chilli sauce and a Kona Longboard lager. Then take the table nearest to the kitchen. Now you are set: when the shrimp arrive you will be consuming the southernmost bar snack in the United States.

42 Foods Tasting Like Another Food

Albatross kebabs	tastes like	Goose kebabs
Chicken	tastes like	Burmese Red Junglefowl
Coca-Koala	tastes like	Pepsi-Koala
Durian fruit (stinking)	tastes like	Raspberry blancmange
Flying fox (fruit bat)	tastes like	Dried bison (dried bison)
Foie gras	tastes like	Pupating silkworm
Frog's legs	taste like	Iguana's legs
Grasshopper	tastes like	Shrimp
Hedgehog	tastes like	Cat
Icelandic rotted shark	tastes like	Gorgonzala
Ortolan buntings*	taste like	Hazelnuts
Pork	tastes like	You
Rhinoceros	tastes like	Kangaroo
Rook crisps	taste like	Grouse crisps
Shearwater (muttonbird)	tastes like	Ewe
Smoked Puffin	tastes like	Smoke
Spam®	tastes like	Spam®
Swan	tastes like	Venison
Tarantula	tastes like	Crab
Truffles	taste like	2,4 dithiapentane
Turtle Soup	tastes like	Gravy
Witchety grubs	taste like	Peanut butter

* Substitute Yellowhammers if the snack cupboard is short of feathered wholefood. Check out local dos and don'ts when choosing species suitable for bird-feeding.

Big Mac. Big Recipe.

Why don't burgers at home taste as good as a Big Mac? Making a facsimile of your favourite burger isn't going to be easy although the thoughtful McDonald's people have put the grocery list up on the interweb. In the UK you will need to lay hands on around 52 ingredients. Here's your list:

UK Big Mac
42 calories per bite*

1) Acetic Acid, 2) Ascorbic Acid, 3) Beef, 4) Butter, 5) Calcium Chloride, 6) Calcium Propionate, 7) Cucumbers, 8) Diphosphates, 9) Dried Garlic, 10) Extractives of Dill, 11) Extractives of other spices, 12) Extractives of Turmeric, 13) Free Range Egg Yolk, 14) Gherkins, 15) Gum Arabic, 16) High-fructose Corn Syrup, 17) Iceberg Lettuce, 18) Milk Proteins, 19) Modified Maize Starch, 20) Mono- and Diacetyl Tartaric Acid Esters of Mono- and Diglycerides of Fatty Acids, 21) Mono- and Diglycerides of Fatty Acids, 22) Mustard Flour, 23) Mustard Seed, 24) Natural Carotenes, 25) Natural Cheese Flavouring, 26) Natural Flavourings, 27) Onion, 28) Palm Oil, 29) Paprika Extract, 30) Pepper, 31) Polyphosphates, 32) Potassium Sorbate, 33) Rapeseed Oil, 34) Salt, 35) Sesame Seeds, 36) Sodium Benzoate., 37) Sodium Stearoyl Lactylate, 38) Sorbic Acid, 39) Soya Flour, 40) Soya Oil, 41) Spice, 42) Spirit Vinegar, 43) Sugar, 44) Trisodium Citrate, 45) Vegetarian Cheddar Cheese, 46) Vinegar, 47) Water, 48) Wheat Fibre, 49) Wheat Flour, 50) Whey Powder, 51) Xanthan Gum, and 52) Yeast

---

* This is at the 11.65 bites per sandwich averaged over the 42 Happy Meals eaten by the Extended Gill family.

DID YOU KNOW? The UK Big Mac is a great source of essential salt, providing some 42% of the recommended daily intake of combined sodium and chlorine ions. By eating two Big Macs and sharing your third one with a friend you are good for a day's salt but still low on those annoying calories. Following this as your daily diet would give a weight loss of six pounds, or more, in just four weeks—and you can drink as much water or other zero-energy beverages as you like, no need to go thirsty.

Bigger and Better

The Big Mac was 42 years old on April 22nd 2009. Jim Delligatti from Pennsylvania sold the first ones for 49 cents in his MacDonald's in Uniontown. Its popularity has enabled *The Economist* magazine to track the buying power of different currencies by comparing Big Mac prices around the world. Your cash will buy fewest Big Macs in Norway, Switzerland and mainland Europe and the most in China, Malaysia and Thailand. Here is the shopping list for a US Big Mac:

US Big Mac
Estimated 46 calories per bite

1) Acetic acid, 2) Ammonium chloride, 3) Ammonium sulfate, 4) Artificial color, 5) Ascorbic acid, 6) Azodicarbonamide, 7) Beef, 8) Black Pepper, 9) Bleached wheat flour, 10) Calcium carbonate, 11) Calcium chloride, 12) Calcium disodium ethylenediaminetetracetic acid, 13) Calcium peroxide, 14) Calcium propionate, 15) Calcium sulfate, 16) Caramel color, 17) Cheese culture, 18) Citric acid, 19) Corn syrup, 20) Cucumbers, 21) Diacetyl tartaric acid ester of monoglyceride, 22) Distilled vinegar, 23) Egg yolks, 24) Enzymes, 25) Ethoxylated monoglycerides, 26) Extractives of paprika, 27) Extractives of turmeric, 28) Folic acid, 29) Garlic powder, 30) Guar gum, 31) High fructose corn syrup, 32) Hydrated potassium aluminum sulfate, 33) Hydrolyzed corn, soy and wheat, 34) Lactic acid, 35) Lettuce, 36) Malted barley flour, 37) Natural flavors (plant source), 38) Milk, 39) Milkfat, 40) Mono- and diglycerides, 41) Monocalcium phosphate, 42) Mustard bran, 43) Mustard seed, 44) Niacin, 45) Onion, 46) Onion powder, 47) Partially hydrogenated soybean oil, 48) Pickles, 49) Polysorbate 80, 50) Potassium sorbate, 51) Propylene glycol alginate, 52) Reduced iron, 53) Riboflavin, 54) Salt, 55) Sesame seed, 56) Sodium benzoate, 57) Sodium citrate, 58) Sodium phosphate, 59) Sodium propionate, 60) Sodium stearoyl lactylate, 61) Sorbic acid, 62) Soy flour, 63) Soy lecithin, 64) Soybean oil, 65) Spice extractives, 66) Spices, 67) Sugar, 68) Thiamin mononitrate, 69) Turmeric, 70) Vinegar, 71) Water, 72) Wheat gluten, 73) Xanthan gum and 74) Yeast.

The US recipe requires 42% more individual ingredients than the UK recipe.

Sport

The First Rule of Cricket

...is that there is no first rule of cricket; cricket has 42 *laws*. The first law prevents the use of 42 fielders, or less specifically all numbers over eleven. Sorry? Your 41 chums had just togged up and are showing all the signs of getting a dose of the glums? Not a problem; just go online—now is good—and book 42 seats to Pago Pago (say 'Pahn-go'; the first or second Pago is either silent or not said) in the South Pacific. Sit back, watch the movie, enjoy your flight, and then rock up for a game of Kirikiti. It sounds like cricket, and it looks a lot like cricket, but it doesn't have the fuss-pot first law limiting team numbers.

Kirikiti has very few laws; no LBW, no offside trap, and neither bad light nor hard rain of the most tropical of intensities stop large teams of both sexes continuing to chat and play, sometimes at the same time, there is no rush. There is little to justify a rush anywhere in Polynesia, especially so in Samoa where Kirikiti is the national game and the proximity of the international dateline makes their bars the last on the planet to announce closing-time. Paradise found for cricket teams of 42.

The Secret of Tennis

42,000 balls were used at Wimbledon last year. This number is considerably less than the estimated two million posters (42cm) that have been sold of 18 year old Fiona Butler apparently forgetfully playing tennis without her knickers. The much-loved picture was taken by her photography student boyfriend Martin Elliott who knew the secret of making really good shots in tennis was to keep the copyright.

Shakespeare with a Bat

The most infamous of times in cricket, known as The Bodyline Series, was caused by an attempt by the England cricket team to contain an Australian sporting genius known as Donald Bradman. The furore started in 1932 when England travelled to play Australia in the fiercely contested biennial Ashes series—the name a mocking reference to the first defeat of mighty England by one of her colonies forty years earlier.

England's captain was Douglas Jardine—born in India to Scottish parents and educated in England at Winchester

College—who developed an unrivalled reputation for stimulating enmity on the cricket field. A talented bat, he had averaged forty-two point something in his rookie international season while touring Australia but also had been seen as a 'snob from England' with an inbuilt Oxford superiority complex drawing antipodean antipathy. When a team-mate helpfully observed that the crowds did not like him, the refined Wykehamist suavely replied, 'It's fucking mutual'.

Jardine and England's problem was a young Australian—Donald Bradman—who had played for Australia in his tenth first class game of cricket and set a record batting average of 139 in the 1930 Ashes Series. The measure of the problem for England is best seen with the benefit of hindsight if you compare best players against second best players across the world's major ball and puck games.

The World's Most Outstanding Ball and Puck Players

Game	Comparing	The best	Superiority	The next best
Cricket	Batting averages	**Sir Don Bradman**	+66%	Sachin Tendulkar*
Golf	'Modern' majors titles	Jack Nicklaus	+29%	Tiger Woods*
Men's Tennis	Slam singles titles	Roger Federer*	+14%	Pete Sampras
Women's Tennis	Slam singles titles	Margaret Court	+9%	Steffi Graf
Soccer	Goals per game	Ferenc Puskas	+5%	Pelé
Baseball	Batting averages	Ty Cobb	+2%	Rogers Hornsby
Ice Hockey	Points per game	Wayne Gretzky	+2%	Mario Lemieux
Football	NFL passer rating	Steve Young	+1%	Philip Rivers*
Basketball	Points per game	Michael Jordan (15 seasons)	=	Wilt Chamberlain (14 seasons)

* Still playing in 2011

He simply lacked peers and was the best player of ball sports since the day the prototype ball rolled off the production line. Surprisingly, 'The Don' is not featured in Malcolm Gladwell's book *Outliers* but his genius is recognised in a book by Australian cricket statman Charles Davis; *The Best of the Best* in which he makes a convincing case that while there would be one Bradman for every 200,000 professional cricketers there would be one Pelé for every 14,000 professional footballers. He sums up Bradman's talent as 'so unlikely it must be described, to paraphrase Douglas Adams, as not impossible, just very, very improbable'.

England's players plotted and came up with the tactic of aiming fast balls at the batsman rather than the wicket he was defending—similar to a beanball in baseball. The English team dressed the tactic with the euphemism of 'fast leg theory' but the Australian media weren't buying euphemisms that day and came up with 'bodyline'. From the start, Jardine instructed his fast bowlers who included the especially quick, Harold Larwood, to go for the man, while he set a special field to take the catches created as batsmen tried to defend themselves from serious injury. This was all within the laws of cricket because until then the idea of propelling a hard ball at 90 mph towards the head or body of an un-helmeted and largely un-padded opponent hadn't been a large part of the original thinking behind the reason everyone had chosen to go out and stand on the grass in the first place. Dissent arose

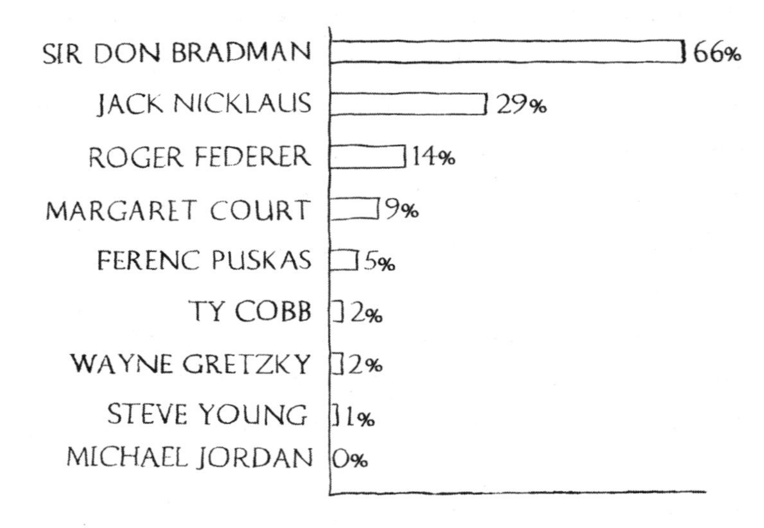

immediately. Gubby Allen refused to follow his captain's bowling instructions and the Nawab of Pataudi refused to field as part of Jardine's leg-trap and was immediately dropped from the side. Few nawabs have played for England since.

Short term, and unsurprisingly, the tactic worked: Bradman hit his lowest ever batting average (still 56) and England won the Ashes. But unprecedented bad feeling had been created within the game of cricket. In an especially heated match in Adelaide, for possibly the first occasion in cricket the crowd booed. A significance for the future diplomatic relationship between the two countries was signalled at government level. The bodyline series and its effects on the game are still spoken of wherever cricketers meet. Bodyline continued to be used by England in the West Indies and in India but after being seen in England by the game's great and good its existence came into question and—possibly under pressure to guarantee that England would not ever bowl bodyline again—Jardine, the England captain, announced his retirement from all cricket.

Sir Don Bradman went on to be famous as the greatest living Australian until his death in 2001, and famous forever as the man whose skill resulted in the changes to law 42 that now protect batsmen from the potentially lethal ferocity of attack that he'd provoked, and faced, as a young cricketer in 1932.

The Texas Game

The national game of Texas is a card game played with dominoes and called 42. It is also played in parts of New Mexico, Oklahoma, Arkansas and Louisiana. The history behind the game is either or both that games involving cards were regarded as immoral by the church or/and that it was illegal to play cards on trains after the Civil War. The game includes a bidding phase in the manner of contract bridge with forty two being the number of points that can be won in a hand of play. It is traditional for US Presidents from Texas to include the playing of 42 on their CV.

The Jackie Robinson Story

By far the world's biggest celebration of the number 42 occurs on 15th April in the United States of America when players, officials and stewards in baseball games around the USA wear Jackie Robinson's Brooklyn Dodgers jersey number in remembrance of the civil rights milestone achieved when Jackie Robinson became the first African-American to play Major League Baseball.

Forbidden to play Major League before 1947, black players had to play in the Negro leagues. Outstanding talents that never got to play at the top level included: Josh Gibson—so good that Babe Ruth was sometimes referred to as the white Josh Gibson, Buck Leonard—the black Lou Gehrig, Judy Johnson—later the first black coach in MLB, Oscar Charleston—rated by some as the greatest ever baseball player, and the mercurially quick Cool Papa Bell—believed to have been quicker than the Olympic sprint champion Jessie Owens.

Even in the army an extraordinarily talented athlete in the America of the 1940s could be subjected to extreme racism. Jackie Robinson had been the first UCLA student to win letters across baseball, football, basketball and track but in the army had had to fight very hard before eventually being accepted for officer training. When he refused to sit in the back of an un-segregrated coach, and objected to blatantly racist military questioning he was given a gerrymandered court-martial but was later fully exonerated and had an honourable discharge. Choosing baseball rather than football or basketball, he was immediately an outstanding new talent, playing professional Negro League in Kansas.

In post-war America the milestone moment for MLB occurred on April 15th 1947 when Jackie Robinson walked out onto Ebbets Field for the Brooklyn Dodgers against the Boston Braves. The colour barrier had been broken, and Jackie Robinson made the first ever MLB Rookie of the Year an African-American. Famous for both the 42 jersey and his sportsmanship, Jackie Robinson played ten MLB seasons and helped win the 1955 World Series. After his diabetes-forced retirement he was the first African-American to be voted into the Baseball Hall of Fame.

The off-field Jackie Robinson was as remarkable as his baseball. In a 1947 poll, Jackie Robinson was the second most popular man in America (after Bing Crosby). In 1950 he played himself in *The Jackie Robinson Story*. He became the first African-American TV analyst and was high profile in promoting opportunities for black Americans. A few weeks before an early death in 1972 the Brooklyn Dodgers retired his number 42 and the following year his wife, Rachel, began the Jackie Robinson Foundation to maintain the legacy and provide scholarships for minority students.

Then in 1997 the unprecedented announcement was made on the fiftieth anniversary of the breaking of the colour barrier that Major League Baseball was retiring Jackie Robinson's jersey number 42 across all teams. The first Jackie Robinson Day was commemorated in 2004 and since 2007 the standing invitation has been for all MLB players on the 15th of April to wear a 42 jersey, maintaining the memory of the times when even a Jackie Robinson could not.

The Astonishing Career of Satchel Paige

No sports story is more remarkable than a top-level career filling some forty years. For many, Leroy 'Satchel' Paige was the best Negro league player of his generation and one of the all-time greatests, but his age appeared to be against his

MLB Player	Year	MLB Season	Age
Barry Bonds	2007	Last	43
Hank Aaron	1976	Last	42
Satchel Paige	**1948**	**First**	**42**
Ty Cobb	1926	Last	41
Babe Ruth	1935	Last	40
Nap Lajoie	1916	Last	40
Yogi Berra	1963	Last	38
Mark McGwire	2001	Last	38
Jackie Robinson	1956	Last	37
Joe DiMaggio	1957	Last	37
Mickey Mantle	1969	Last	37

following Jackie Robinson ('the greatest colored player I've ever seen', said Satchel in a cleverly diplomatic comparison) into Major League Baseball. But such was his potential to draw the crowds (DiMaggio called Paige the best pitcher he'd ever faced) that on the day of his 42nd birthday he signed with the Cleveland Indians. A $40,000 three month contract made him the first Negro pitcher in MLB, two days later walking onto the pitch and making one baseball statistic that is now truly unbeatable: the oldest MLB rookie.

Three weeks later a record was set for a major league night game when a crowd of 72,562 appeared to see Paige pitching. The Cleveland Indians won the 1948 World Series, although Paige played a relatively minor part. He was to continue pitching in MLB and Triple-A baseball until 1966. By then he was an incredible sixty years old and in 1971 he was the first African-American pitcher to be inducted into the Baseball Hall of Fame.

The Magician

Chicken, steak, pork, lamb and alcohol are not dietary requirements for sporting legendhood. Sir Stanley Matthews the English soccer player was an abstemious vegetarian who used amazing pace and ball-dribbling skills with ruthless effect to beat defenders and win the name of '*The Magician*' from fans. Playing around 800 games, he was never booked for misconduct in an English league career lasting from 1932 until 1965, retiring he said 'too early' at the age of 50. Most of his club career was with Stoke and Blackpool, where he helped win the 1953 FA Cup in a game called the Matthews Final, the only final ever to be associated with one man. He made 54 official England appearances and played in 29 'unofficial' games during WWII. He was the oldest player ever to have scored for England at the age of 41 in 1957 and when he was 42, became the oldest England player with the longest ever England career.

PS (Previously Secret)

Secret records released from the public record office in 2010 under the sixty year rule included the details of an incident in 1945 in which Corporal Matthews and his friend Aircraftman Stan 'Electric Heels' Mortensen (who had survived a bomber crash and later became the only player ever to score three goals in an FA Cup final—the Matthews final) were involved in a spot of bother. Having helped beat Belgium 3-2 in an unofficial England game as an Armed Services International XI, the international soccer stars walked into a Brussels shop carrying a suitcase with a view to selling coffee and soap in the manner of Private Walker from *Dad's Army*. It is a reasonably safe guess that England's finest footballers did not then have the phone numbers of agents capable of demanding the 1945 equivalent of the £6,500,000 club salaries of England's World Cup 2010 heroes Steven Gerrard, Frank Lampard and John Terry, players who should perhaps be now considering vegetarianism and teetotalism as a means of making the team in 2014.

The Father of Baseball. A Brit

I am pleased to relate that the inventor of the mostly harmless pastime of baseball statistics was English. Sensing a need for numbers, Henry Chadwick left England's bucolic West Country in an unlikely quest to enliven America. As a journalist in New York he could see that the young nation really needed to be making box scores, calculating batting averages, computing an earned run average and have at least one good man keeping a sharp eye on runs batted in. First, he needed Americans outdoors, preferably playing a game of some kind rather than standing aimlessly on corners. Chadwick was the man America had been waiting for—understanding that England had cricket he chose baseball as an all-American sport that would guarantee the statistics the country needed. Promoting baseball through his columns he also worked on rules that would help create more statistics, all the time scrupulously noting everything that moved, or might move at some stage. By 1860 he had what would set America on her way: the first book of baseball stats being nattily entitled *Beadle's Dime Base-Ball Player*.

Aged 42 he was scoring for the National Baseball Club of Washington D.C. on their first national tour and continued his life in baseball until his death. Henry Chadwick is one of three Englishmen in the Baseball Hall of Fame and the only baseball writer. His grave marker reads 'Father of baseball'.

The 42-42 Club

Henry Chadwick knew America's secret desire. Baseball boasts, as I write, 6247 different performance statistics. It doesn't, I just made that up but there are an extraordinarly vast number and until baseball statistics receive proper attention 6247 will do as a highly plausible quantum. There are almost certainly more statistics relating to baseball than any other sport, there are university courses on baseball stats and WikiProject Baseball scores Wikpedia baseball articles by quality and importance; at this moment the project is keeping tabs on 33,438 pages.

The most fun to be had is in synthesising a new statistic. Here are two from Shropshire in England: firstly, players batting .42 or better in a season.

MLB Player	Season	Batting Average
Hugh Duffy	1894	.440
Tip O'Neill	1887	.435
Ross Barnes	1876	.429
Nap Lajoie	1901	.426
Willie Keeler	1897	.424
Rogers Hornsby	1924	.424
Ty Cobb	1911	.420
George Sisler	1922	.420

Since the most recent occasion fans saw a major-leaguer player bat .42 in a season was 1924 I think we need something more topical: the 42-42 Club. This is a neo-stat being two notches beyond the 40-40 Club. Membership is achieved by hitting 42 home runs and stealing 42 bases in a season. There is one guy in the club-house so far—Alex Rodriguez, with the Seattle Mariners in the '98 season he hit 42 home runs and stole 46 bases. A player purloining this many bases on this kind of basis will have soon filled the garage and be over-spilling into the yard.

1966 And All That

The result of the most famous game in English football was 4-2. And its most famous match official was Tofic Bahkramov, the Azerbaijan linesman (most definitely not 'Russian') who persuaded the referee that England's third goal in the 1966 World Cup final between England and Germany was good. In Germany they still aren't seeing it the same way, a shot that hits the bar then the goal line is, saracastically, now a 'Wembley goal'.

Tofic became the first FIFA official to officiate at two World Cups and was a national hero for his work promoting both football and Azerbaijan. The national stadium in capital Baku bears his name and British prime minister Margaret Thatcher asked to meet him on a visit in 1992. Perhaps the ultimate tribute was paid in 2004 when the scorer of the first 'Wembley goal', Sir Geoff Hurst, unveiled a statue of the linesman who played a part in his World Cup hat-trick. It is probably the world's only monument celebrating a linesman.

The Gold Retriever

The England team's presentation with the World Cup was thanks to Pickles, a mongrel dog, who supposedly was allowed to lick the plates at the after-match celebration. Recognisable around the world, the Jules Rimet trophy not Pickles, vanished while on display at a convention of stamp collectors. Fortunately for England it was scented out from under a hedge a few days afterwards by Pickles. If I am swivelling my complimentary patented Duckworth-Lewis Rubik cube correctly it appears that in human years, Pickles was 42 (D/L method).

In a bad case of history failing to repeat itself, after being won outright by Brazil in 1970 the Jules Rimet trophy vanished for a second time in 1983. It is feared that this time it was smelted not smelt.

The First 42 Ks Are The Worst

A marathon course is now set at 42 kilometres and 195 metres. Give or take 42 metres. This became the official course length in 1921 having varied since the first modern race in 1896. The first 42k marathon had been run 13 years earlier at the 1908 London Olympics—being the distance from Windsor Castle to the Olympic White City stadium. The race is remembered because it was the first Olympics with significant surviving film and was especially famous because the first man over the line, the Italian Dorando Peitri had had to be helped and was disqualified in favour of the second-placed American.

To allow Queen Alexandra the best view of the finish the direction of the final lap of the stadium was reversed from the anti-clockwise common at most sports tracks. Dorando entered the stadium but turned right, confused and totally exhausted his final 385 yards before crossing the line was to take ten minutes. The film had made the marathon popular and Dorando went on to make significant earnings by finishing first in two re-runs staged in America with the gold medal winner.

Art and Literature

The Defining Genius

One of few London houses built around 1700 and still standing, 17 Gough Square, was the place where 42-year-old Samuel Johnson was living and working when mid-way through the task of compiling his world-famous *Dictionary of the English Language.* It is regarded as one of the greatest works of scholarly genius ever. It was the first dictionary to reveal how a language worked, Johnson's insight was to choose for each word phrases and sentences that made exemplary use of the word. In a nine year period he defined a total of 42,777 words with 114,000 illustrative examples.

Not allowing for duvet-days, Johnson defined an average of 15 words per day. Having agreed a price in advance for a task he had expected to take three years he found himself working for an unexpected six further years, ending up receiving the equivalent of 9 old pence per word defined. In terms of equivalent buying power in 2011 he was getting £90 a day but from this he still had to pay his assistants. The lexicographical genius was working at close to today's minimum wage.

Now Turn to Page 42

On the June 30th 1997 a children's book by JK Rowling called *Harry Potter and the Philosopher's Stone* was published. On page 42 Harry Potter discovers he is a wizard. The idea caught and the seventh and final Harry Potter was completed on January 11th 2007 on the sixth floor (the seventh floor if you are a US citizen) of the Balmoral Hotel in Edinburgh. Later in the same year a copy of JK Rowling's *Beedle the Bard* became the most expensive modern manuscript when it was bought at auction in London for £1.95 million. JK Rowling was 42.

Also on Page 42*

Dracula, Bram Stoker	Jonathan Harker discovers he is imprisoned in his oddish host's Transylvanian castle.
Frankenstein, Mary Shelley	Victor Frankenstein reveals he is able to create life.
Robinson Crusoe, Daniel Defoe	After leaving Hull in the early 17th century, about as late as one would want to sensibly leave it, his ship runs aground on a desert island during a hurricane. Last known latitude was in 12° 18'. So the island may have been Tobago, or Grenada, or Barbados, or none of them.
The Hitch-hiker's Guide to the Galaxy, Douglas Adams	Hero, Arthur Dent, discovers he is hitch-hiking on a spacecraft of the Vogon Constructor Fleet. The BBC had turned down the idea of developing a book from the radio series.
Treasure Island, Robert Louis Stevenson	Blind Pew checks out having been trampled by horses as recently as page 41

* Of the first editions

The Whale

In 2008 Frank Mundus spent a last night on the *Cricket II* at anchor in Lake Montauk, New York before flying home to Big Island, Hawai'i. He never reached home, dying from a heart attack in Honolulu airport. Until his death he had maintained that he and his forty-two foot boat had been the inspiration for Peter Benchley's character Quint in the novel *Jaws*. It was true that Frank Mundus had harpooned a 4500lb-ish shark (never weighed) and that the *Jaws* author had been on his shark-fishing trips but it is Captain Ahab and the white whale, Moby Dick, that ring truer in any search for the origins of the lonely character of Quint and his never named nemesis and the original screenplay for *Jaws* had even planned to have the film open with Quint watching *Moby Dick* in the cinema but this required the permission of Gregory Peck who had been unhappy with his performance as Ahab and declined.

Much of Herman Melville's inspiration for *Moby-Dick* was real life. Discourses dealing with everything-you-wanted-to-know-about-whaling-but-hadn't-known-to-enquire came from time working on a New Bedford whaler. There was a very real Moby Dick; an issue of a New York magazine published two years before Melville joined the whaler in 1841 had a feature article about a notably aggressive white whale off the coast of Chile known well to the whaling crews who called the beast Mocha Dick. And the boatload of allegories that stemmed from a ship and her frail human crew abroad in an alien world being destroyed by the wild creature they were hunting came from Owen Chase, who had written a narrative of his experience in the shipwreck of the *Essex*, the Nantucket whaler sunk in 1820 by a large sperm whale. Only eight *Essex* men returned, having eaten seven shipmates to survive. (The aural adrenalin that is Mountain's song *Nantucket Sleighride (To Owen Coffin)* is also partly about the *Essex*. A Nantucket sleighride was a metaphor used to describe the sensation of being in a small whaleboat as it was towed at speed by a harpooned whale, and Owen Coffin had been a seventeen-year-old on the *Essex* who, having survived the attack, was in a small boat when he drew the black spot to be killed and eaten by three others including his cousin…a family meal.) *Moby-Dick* took years to become a treasure of world literature, not selling its initial print run of books now worth $100,000 each and Herman Melville died unrecognised as a great writer, never to know that his choice and ordering of words had formed a Great American Novel.

There have been five films, nine if you include the *Jaws* family. When small I remember my parents taking me with my brother and sister aboard the *Pequod* to walk on the deck where Ahab, Starbuck, Ishmael and Queequeg had stood beside cauldrons of flensed blubber. This was the ship used in the 1956 film, making her final bow as a visitor attraction in Morecambe in North-west England and where—having slipped the attentions of a giant squid and an albino cetacean—fire did for in 1972.

Ein Augenblick later and we are with our own children on a different boat when suddenly and terrifyingly a Great White Shark rears from the water towards our craft. It is the *Jaws* ride at Universal Studios Florida where the excited screams show no-one's getting bored anytime soon of Steven Spielberg's adaptation of Peter Benchley's drawing on Herman Melville's use of Owen Chase's original telling of the real-life story of the *Essex*.

Audubon's Birds

Aged 42 in 1827, JJ Audubon published *Birds of America*, the greatest picture book ever produced. Printed in Britain, the 435 39 inches by 26 inches hand-coloured prints cost $115,640 (estimated at over $2m in 2011) and had originally been sold by subscription, five plates at a time being delivered in 87 tinned cases. His working method comprised starting at 3am to spend the morning hunting specimens and working late into each evening painting. All the paintings are remarkable in being life-size—an eagle apparently taking 60 hours to paint. While in Edinburgh, Scotland the young Charles Darwin went to a lecture by Audubon about his methods.

119 complete copies of the Double Elephant Folio exist and the most recent one to change ownership was bought at auction in London for $11.5m in 2010. It had been owned by Baron Hesketh's family and the price was the highest ever for a printed book. Plate 42 features the Orchard Oriole.

The Gutenberg Bible

B42 is the world's most expensive book, valued at £20 million if a copy was sold it is also known as the 42-line bible from the 42 lines of type on each page, and the Gutenberg Bible because it was printed by Johannes Gutenburg. The book started the printing revolution by being the first to be known to be printed with moveable type. The press was known to be in operation in 1451 in the German city of Mainz, then a part of the Holy Roman Empire and where the university is named for their famous printer. The first print run of 150 incunable bibles (incunabula is your word for the day, being books and other printed material dated on or before 1500) was to sell out and Johannes Gutenberg is now widely regarded as one of the most influential people of the past 1000 years. 'What the world is today, good and bad, we owe to Gutenberg' wrote Mark Twain—for whom financial happiness did not follow literary triumph, losing a large part of his fortune investing in a new typesetting machine and some of the rest in attempting to become a publisher. Despite declaring bankruptcy to escape the debacle he embarked on a world lecture tour and successfully repaid his creditors.

For Gutenberg financial happiness did not follow technical triumph. He had borrowed to fund the work until the sets of printed pages (not bound) could be sold. With the Bible finished and selling, his lender then sued on what might well have been spurious grounds and won most of Gutenberg's assets including the commercially magical printing press—which he immediately cranked up again to make very saleable printed books.

Over half a millennium on and Project Gutenberg represents a new print revolution, the free distribution of e-books out of copyright in the United States. In 2010 the top ten downloaded authors were:

1. Sir Arthur Conan Doyle
2. Mark Twain
3. Charles Dickens
4. Jane Austen
5. William Shakespeare
6. Sir Richard Francis Burton
7. Lewis Carroll
8. Vatsyayana (The Kama Sutra)
9. Jules Verne
10. H. G. Wells

The Genuine Goldfinger

The champion Canadian-bred wonder horse Nijinsky (Nijinsky II in the US) was 42 months old in 1970 when he became the last horse to win the three races called the English Triple Crown; the Derby, the 2000 Guineas and the St Leger. Sensationally at the time the nag and his jockey Lester Piggott then lost by a head in the French Arc de Triomphe, shortly afterwards being retired and syndicated to stud for a world record amount. Nijinsky's fame and popular appeal resulted in a documentary film, narrated by Orson Welles, being shown in UK cinemas. In 2000 Nijinsky was voted the horse of the millennium.

His owner was the sensationally wealthy Charles W. Englehardt Jr. on whom the Ian Fleming character of *Goldfinger* is almost certainly part-based. Engelhardt had been a friend of Ian Fleming since 1947 and was known as the 'Platinum King', also having legally exported gold from South Africa as objects of art to be turned back into ingots, a manoeuvre echoed in the novel.

Played by Gert Fröbe in the film, card-cheat Auric

Goldfinger is a favourite Fleming villain and was given the precise age of 42 years old—exactly the same age as Charles W. Engelhardt Jr. when the first edition of *Goldfinger* came out in March 1959.

Excellent Science

Calling Elvis

12 hours before the death of Elvis Presley a large steel grid 500 miles away from Graceland and 1250 miles from Roswell detected the only signal ever to be considered a contender for having come from life elsewhere in the universe. Elvis reportedly lead a nocturnal life and bedtimes in the Presley household could be as early as six o'clock in the morning. On the morning of the August 16th 1977 Elvis hadn't managed to nod off and so went to another room to read a new book he was interested in called *A Scientific Search for the Face of Jesus*.

The scientific search for extra-terrestrial life had started in the early sixties and tried to detect radio signals from space. One theory was that such a signal would be sent using the radio wavelength of the literally universal phenomenon know as the hydrogen line; a frequency of 1420 MHz which is the signature of the element hydrogen that makes up three-quarters of all the matter in the universe.

The chance of detecting a vanishingly faint radio transmission increases if you go super-size with your aerial. One of 34,000 square feet was constructed in 1963, in a moment of high drollery called Big Ear, and was set to work scanning all the sky that can be heard from Delaware, Ohio. The skyscan identified over 20,000 natural radio emitters including superstars of the universe—quasars equalling a trillion suns each. Very exciting but definitely not lifelike and nothing else was either. After 14 years of hoping, everyone had gone home leaving just the computer to watch over stuff on the night of the August 15th 1977, which was exactly when stuff happened—a clear signal at 1420 MHz that lasted 72 seconds, making a hill on a graph as the earth turned her

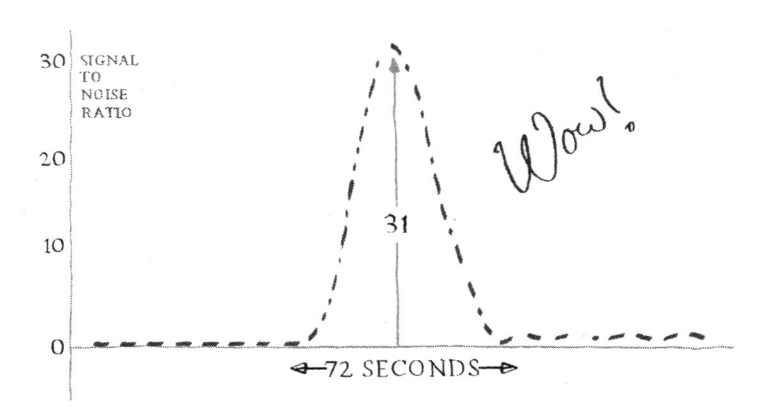

giant lug towards, directly at, and then away from a radio source apparently somewhere in distant space.

This was to be the strongest signal of unexplained origin the radio telescope ever detected in 34 years. It was right on the 1420 MHz mark and it was purely on the 1420 MHz mark—natural radio sources generally have a mess of different frequencies. The signal ended and that was it. It reads 6-E-Q-U-J-5 but this was nothing sentient, being just six signal strength readings over a period of 72 seconds yet the six were so different to anything the guys in Ohio had ever seen that Dr Jerry Ehrman—the scientist checking the readout—wrote 'Wow!' in the margin alongside the signal.

The mystery status of the 'Wow! Signal' has never altered. It had appeared to come from an empty area of space alongside M55, a fuzzball of 20,000 plus stars located in the constellation of Sagittarius (one of the fire signs—compatible with Aries). But there is nothing there to hear or see—it's just, space. Numerous attempts have been made to find another signal: none has succeeded. Elvis Presley never came back from the other room, he died there with his book within twelve hours of Big Ear picking up The Wow! Signal. Within a hundred days Steven Spielberg's *Close Encounters of the Third Kind* was released. And Douglas Adams was in Stalbridge, Dorset, England writing

The Hitch-hiker's Guide to The Galaxy—to be broadcast as radio signals.

Big Ear didn't ever hear a second signal and the land was eventually made over into a golf course. The next time a message from advanced life on another planet bridges the unimaginable voids of space it will reach a golfer.

One Small Fall

Shapes with three sides you will recall from school. The isosceles triangle had two sides identical, the scalene triangle hadn't any identical sides, and the...sit up, please...the Bermuda Triangle is the one that changed shape every time a new book got written about it. Authors have even upped the number of sides in a triangle to as many as seven. This was the famous Bermuda Irregular Heptagon you may have missed reading about.

Locales to have made it into Bermuda 'Triangles' have included: Texas, Mexico, the whole Caribbean, Cuba, North Carolina, Barbados and from deep left Atlantic; the Azores archipelago, which might be in Europe but is sort of close to the sighting of the *Mary Celeste* and easily worth a chapter in any book.

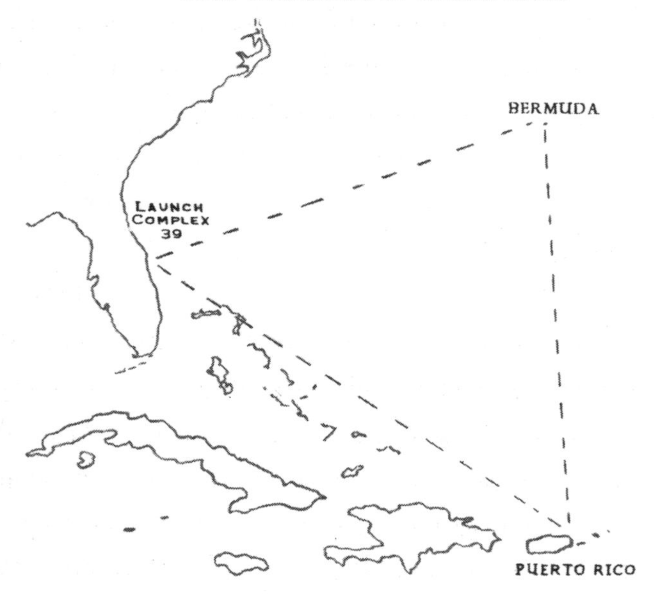

A tale every bit as queer as that of the deserted *Mary Celeste* relates to the very illustration above. Needing to see the best scale to draw the map and lettering I wanted a book of just the right size to compare my triangle of Bermuda against—adding here that my books are not catalogued to Dewey decimal points of precision: any book could be in any toilet at any time, at night I sometimes think I can hear them moving about—and so with a draft triangle to hand I pulled a suitably dimensioned paperback from a shelf. It was an old book that I'd quite forgotten I possessed. The book was Charles Berlitz's *The Bermuda Triangle*. Eyes invariably widen every time I'm in Tesco's and volunteer this true tale to a checkout operator in a forlorn attempt to fill the conversational vacuum that follows the revelation that I have, once again, left the home *sans* clubcard.

This book's Bermuda Triangle joins the islands of Bermuda and Puerto Rico with Merritt Island, on which is NASA's Launch Complex 39 and near to Cape Canaveral. After 24 successful launches from pad A, in January 1986 the shuttle *Challenger* set out on its tenth mission by being the first to travel the 4.2 miles from the shuttle assembly building to pad B, from where it launched but exploded seconds later. In 2003 pad A was used by the shuttle *Columbia* which was to disintegrate on returning to Earth. Pad A had also been used by Apollo 13 in 1970. The story of Apollo 13's heroic return from a near fatal incident in space is well known, especially because of the excellent Tom Hanks' film, but perhaps less familiar are details of the events that came so close to causing a horrible disaster.

Storing oxygen sufficient for three men over ten days in a small volume meant liquefying oxygen gas down into a slush that needed to be kept extremely cold (under minus two hundred degrees centigrade) in two spherical tanks. Inside each tank was an electric heater and stirrer fans used to warm and mix the slush back into breathable oxygen. This had all worked successfully on six previous manned Apollo missions but, as Richard Feynman was to write in his highly personal addendum to the later *Challenger* shuttle enquiry, assuming there was some kind of parity between previous non-failures and future safety should be considered seriously flawed thinking.

The Apollo mission's meticulous enquiry discovered that one of the two tanks had been accidentally dropped, just two inches, a year earlier. The fall appeared to have damaged the internal pipe that was used to fill the tank and empty the tank during pre-flight testing. Before the mission a problem had arisen emptying one of the tanks. This was probably a result of the fall. The work-around to empty the tank was to switch on the heater which would evaporate off the remaining liquid. This alone would not have been a problem but for a second unfortunate occurrence.

The original electrics in each tank were designed for 28 volts of electricity to match the voltage of the Apollo spacecraft, but for flexibility during mission preparation they were retro-adapted to also function on the 65 volt Cape Canaveral system. An 'oversight' meant that the original 28 volt thermostats, there to prevent overheating by switching off the current at a set temperature, weren't adapted and received 65 volts for eight hours. The result was that the thermostats became welded into their 'on' position. A temperature gauge on the tank had a maximum reading of 26°C so couldn't register the extent of the problem but the thermostat failures were reckoned to have caused the temperature to have gone over 500°C. This amount of heat melted electrical insulation on parts of the wiring to the stirrer fan. Because the thermostats were now always 'on' the heater would work whenever it was needed so no problem was detected before the mission.

The explosion-in-waiting happened on the third occasion that the tank's stirrer fans were used during the mission. The bare stirrer fan wires sparked, setting plastic insulation alight in pure oxygen which increased the pressure and then exploded the oxygen tank causing almost catastrophic damage to surrounding equipment including the second oxygen tank. The astronauts felt a jolt and their electrics suddenly started to die: immediately it was a serious situation. A few seconds later forty-two year old mission commander, James Lovell, confirmed to Houston mission control that they'd 'had' a problem. A small fall for one component a year before had just caused a giant problem on a spacecraft 200,000 miles from Earth in the form of cascading vital system failures. Multiple simultaneous system failure had not been part of the astronauts' many practice drills. It was considered too unlikely.

Warning: Triangles

The United States Coast Guard is frequently asked about the Bermuda Triangle. Their website makes everything clear: 'The Coast Guard does not recognize the existence of the so-called Bermuda Triangle as a geographic area of specific hazard to ships or planes.' So, official US Government advice is that ***ALL TRIANGLES*** are considered to be equally hazardous to navigation (my underlined, emboldened, sloping, capital letters, this is important). The last statement can be tested as scientifically as you like by comparing the Bermuda Triangle with other triangles. I will choose just one, The Roswell Triangle, but if you are even mildly sceptical you should run a similar comparison with your own favourite triangles.

The Roswell Triangle runs across eleven States including parts of the South and mid-America, going from Roswell, New Mexico to Graceland in Memphis, and thence up to Delaware, Ohio—where 'The Wow! Signal' was received either just possibly or absolutely definitely having been sent by aliens (page 149).

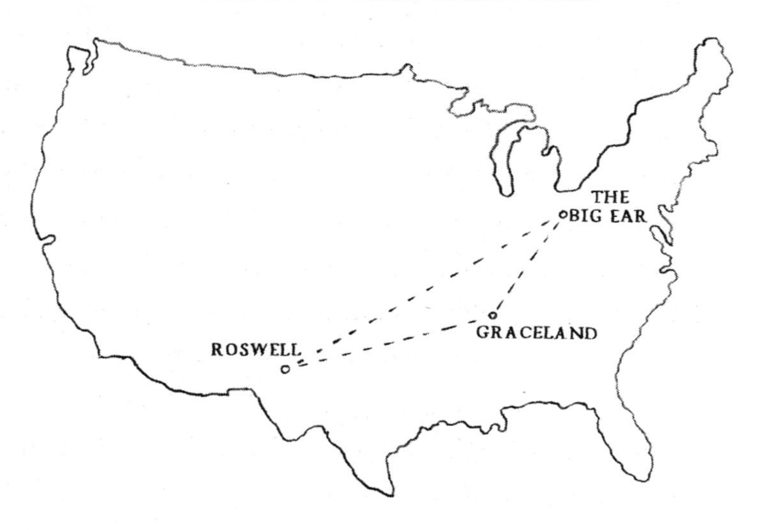
THE ROSWELL TRIANGLE
THE
BIG EAR
GRACELAND
ROSWELL

	Bermuda Triangle	Roswell Triangle
Mainly	Ocean	Land
Area	350,000 square nautical miles and upwards	120,000 square miles
Aircraft lost	130+. Reported ditchings or disappearances	1095+. All fatal crashes, almost all being individual light aircraft
Great lighthouse incidents	1 The Great Isaac Lighthouse incident, In 1969 the two Bahamian keepers were found to have just disappeared	0
Worst nautical loss of life	306 dead The collier USS *Cyclops* carrying ore and passengers, disappeared somewhere between Barbados and Baltimore in 1918. Not confirmed as having sunk in The Bermuda Triangle	1800 dead (estimated) The third greatest disaster in United States history after 9/11 and Pearl Harbour. The greatly overcrowded SS *Sultana* suffered a boiler explosion on the Mississippi river just north of Memphis near submerged island 42 in the late evening of 27th April 1865. Those who died mostly comprised Civil War prisoners of war returning home to the North The number of deaths was around 300 greater than the number lost on the RMS *Titanic*

Who knew? America's third biggest disaster occurred as far inland as the RMS *Titanic* was offshore, around 350 miles. No-one had known how many soldiers had boarded the Sultana, and none of them were rich or famous and it would be hard to imagine more competing news—being comparable in contemporary terms to the simultaneous ending of the Second World War and President Kennedy being murdered quickly followed by Lee Harvey Oswald being murdered.

When the SS *Sultana* exploded in late April 1865, the four year American Civil War had just ended, confusedly, over a period of days that included John Wilkes Booth's killing of President Lincoln. Booth escaped and had been on the run for two weeks when news of his being shot at a farmstead in Virginia was the headline on the day the SS *Sultana* sank. The country could be said to be in a state of confusion and shock, the newspapers being filled with the stories of the ending of the war, the President's assassination and of the crowds still gathering to pay their respects to Lincoln's body at the towns where the train carrying the coffin was halting in a two week journey from Washington to Springfield, Illinois. The deaths of the people on the SS *Sultana* weren't as newsworthy, and so sank with little trace.

The Tumbleweed Men

'Camera.'

'Doh!'

Larry loosed a hand from the DS and tapped the Big Red Stop Button which—following a neat exhibition of soldering-iron work by Sergey—now simultaneously muted *Bohemian Rhapsody* on the camera car's funky retro eight-track. The 42 from Albuquerque had brought the Google guys into Corona, New Mexico. She was a hot one. Two locals tasked to the tumbleweed blower on Main Street were turning HTML #FF0000*.

'Say, do you know where we could get a couple of good green chile cheese burgers?' yelled Larry over the hum of a Pratt & Whitney TF33 turbofan jet engine that the small town had enterprisingly salvaged from a surplus B-52 Stratofortress.

---

* Pantone® 1795 C♠

♠ Lobster red mainly

Two fingers were slowly raised directing them to a low building that seemed an insufficiently grand design to support a freshly-painted and unmissably large sign that read: 'Good Green Chile Cheese Burgers'. Waiting for a gap in the Mach 1 tumbleweeds Larry and Sergey crossed the road and once inside gave involuntary air-con shivers as they stood absorbing the sights and smells of another fast-food paradise.

'Hello, Dave,' rasped a voice from back in the kitchen followed by the appearance of a sharp dressed man with an Elvis quiff and aviator glasses who neither apologised nor explained away the curious greeting, instead placing on the counter the *Albuquerque Tribune* and returning their gaze in mirrored lenses.

Sergey ordered two Corona Specials. On the radio a local station was reporting excitedly on a big basketball derby; the Albuquerque Grays were a short nose ahead of The Roswell Incidents at 43 to 41. Larry headed for an empty booth with the newspaper, it seemed that Corona had made the front page, below the fold:

CORONA COUNTER-COUNTER-CONSPIRACY FACILITY DENIAL TO BE CONFIRMED BY CIA

The CIA issued a press release today (10/10/10) stating that a statement is expected confirming the denial of the existence of the CIA Corona Counter-Counter-Conspiracy Facility (Area 2a).

The bulletin will probably reveal that the government's Corona Enquiry has found that the small town of Corona in New Mexico is a small town in New Mexico and has never been a front for the world's leading source of supply for mis-mis-information.

Corona's non-connection with the CIA didn't start in 1947 when a local rancher drove into town and told of finding a weather balloon in the desert, fourteen days earlier the world's first ever flying saucer had been reported over Idaho. Within hours a call had been put in to the Air Force at Roswell saying that what looked like a crashed alien spacecraft had been found 42 miles north-west of the secret atomic airbase and that rushing out an official military press release describing the incident by using the word 'disc' at least four times would be an outstanding idea.

Sergey brought over the burgers that were, like, totally historic; each being quite large enough to have been served on its own tectonic plate. Happily refuelled, the Google guys stepped out into the heat to continue their epic mission to film America. Larry clicked on the Motorola to catch the basketball result. Strange, the station wasn't there now. Pulling an iPad from the rear seat he googled the game:

> ⚠ No results found for "Albuquerque Grays v The Roswell Incidents".

Whoa. Sergey tried the *Albuquerque Tribune's* website: a journalist's last lament told of a circulation of 42,000 copies twenty years earlier but that February 20, 2008 was to be the final issue and that no further newspapers would ever be published. Double Whoa. The Google guys decided it was time to leave Corona. 'Camera,' reminded Sergey as they pulled away.

The tumbleweed men removed their sunglasses and stared at the sedan until it was a small dot disappearing in the inhuman heat of the New Mexico desert. Their lidless eyes had never blinked.

Real Stardust

The element molybdenum has the atomic number of 42 and is also the 42nd most common element in the universe. This isn't a pleasing coincidence; most of the stuff in the universe is truly ancient hydrogen and helium that has existed since almost the time of Big Bang. Hydrogen and helium are the lightest elements with atomic numbers 1 and 2. Everything heavier such as the elements for making fingernails or aircraft carriers got formed later within stars which shone, burnt out, and got recycled. The way this process works generally means there is less and less of each element according to its atomic number.

Molybdenum is an element of surprises. It has the fifth highest melting point of 2632 degrees centigrade and DIY drill bits are made of molybdenum-rich steel. It is also needed within enzymes used by all animals, all plants and most bacteria. You would be dead without the five milligrams of molybdenum your body contains.

The isotope of calcium known as ^{42}Ca has an isotopic mass of almost exactly 42. There is nothing else of interest to be gleaned from ^{42}Ca, please pass on to the next exhibit.

Eye of newt & toe of frog

'It's impossible to travel faster than the speed of light, and certainly not desirable, as one's hat keeps blowing off.'

Woody Allen

Hawking wrote that for every equation he employed the readership of *A Brief History of Time* would halve—and proceeded to find space for one equation for his nine million book-buyers. This was the equation keeping the brake on book sales:

$$E = mc^2$$

The world's most famous equation is from Einstein's theory of special relativity. In a fun book, *Why Does $E=mc^2$?* Professors Brian Cox and Jeff Forshaw of Manchester University answer the nontrivial question of their title—along the way including a request to readers to remember Douglas Adams' 'Don't Panic' message from *The Hitch-hiker's Guide to the Galaxy*. Despite the 'equals' sign positioned centre stage E-equals-mc-squared really means that energy and mass are two forms of one thing and that energy is always conserved. Energy leaving matter removes mass from it, and energy joining matter adds mass to it. But with *c* standing in for the speed of light* and which is promptly self-multiplied the numbers are—as Douglas Adams described space—vastly, hugely and mind-bogglingly big.

If you take *just one gram of mass* (*m*), and I see you have selected the eye of a newt and the toe of a frog, then you also the seemingly unbelievable equivalent of the energy (*E*) that would be the result of the simultaneous explosion of *42 million sticks of dynamite*. Taking the mass of the ink in the full-stop at the end of this sentence, and just taking the ink not the paper underneath please, it contains the potential explosive power of approximately 12 sticks of dynamite, which should be a good reason for knowing the best way to handle punctuation. Having safely read the aforementioned terminal mark I can tell you that it didn't explode under normal reading conditions because virtually all of the energy is to be found in the force that keeps atoms as atoms (it had been believed within living memory that it was impossible to split the atom).

---

* Which moves a distance equal to 42 trips between New York and Rome in one second.

Non-nuclear explosions don't split atoms. When dynamite explodes, exotic, easily excited nitroglycerine molecules rearrange their atoms into plainer and steadier molecules: oxygen, nitrogen, water, and carbon dioxide. Despite the trauma not a single atom would have been harmed, or found to be missing or have changed into a different element. Measure the mass before & after and you will find there is a shortfall after the blast. From 42 million sticks that shortage would be a gram—the energy released in the explosion.

It is impossible, today, but if amphibian body part matter could be converted wholly into energy then the opposite is the case—not a single atom would remain. All would have become notional ex-atoms. The universe would be one gram short of the elements comprising newt and frog and would possess an additional gram of heat and electromagnetic radiation mass. Other matter, anything, could absorb the heat and the radiation and gain one gram in the mass of its matter. If the universe were a person, she just can't lose weight.

In 1945 the world's third man-made nuclear explosion destroyed much of the north of a Japanese city, Nagasaki. It ended the Second World War but killed some 70,000 people and caused injury, disease and suffering for many more. When Fat Man detonated, an estimated 1200 grams of synthesised plutonium metal changed into 1199 grams of other elements. The death and suffering of Nagasaki was caused by the single gram of energy released with the destructive power of 42 million sticks of dynamite.

And Last Year's Winner Is

The German physicist recognised as the world's greatest scientist, Albert Einstein, received the Nobel Physics Prize for the year 1921 when he was 42, although his prize wasn't announced until late in 1922 when the 1922 physics prize was announced simultaneously in the same breath.

The prize had followed headlines in 1919 that observations made during a solar eclipse had confirmed Einstein's prediction that light from a star would be seen to be bent by the Sun's gravity. Relativity still being a hot topic for debate the Nobel prize was deliberately not linked to e-equals-mc-squared. It was more of a lifetime achievement award with special mention of discovery of the law of a phenomenon known as the photoelectric effect. This introduced the photon to the world as the then accepted answer to the tough question of how light could pull off a trick that made it appear to be a wave and a particle in the same instant. Digital cameras are a direct result of Einstein's work here.

It seems most surprising today to learn that for a further 17 years after first writing e-equals-mc-squared even Albert Einstein didn't know that it meant incredible amounts of energy could be released from matter. That insight required the thinking of a younger man. Further knowledge on the structure of atoms had been gained and in 1923 Enrico Fermi, an Italian scientist working at Pisa University, was the first to see that within e-equals-mc-squared lay the potential for nuclear energy. A modest man of great genius, it was Enrico Fermi who first knew that the world would begin a nuclear age rather than Albert Einstein. Ironically, Fermi was to die aged 53 from stomach cancer caused by having worked without sufficient protection close to sources of radiation.

Crime, Mystery, and Disaster

Doggo, or Dead?

Between four and eight am on Friday, November 8th 1974 a motorist parked a dark grey Ford Corsair fitted with a roof-rack near 42 Norman Road, Newhaven, West Sussex. After putting the keys in the glove box, he walked down Norman Road into one of the greatest mysteries of modern times.

'Lucky' Lord Lucan was a 39 year old English aristocrat known as John to his many friends. He had just murdered, according to the last inquest jury ever permitted to deliver such a verdict, Mrs Sandra Rivett, the 29-year-old single mother newly employed as nanny to his children, in what appeared to be a case of mistaken identity; his intended victim was possibly their mother with whom he was embroiled in an embittered divorce—he had mistakenly believed that Sandra Rivett would be out of the house on her regular night off.

Lord Lucan's body has never been found. His alibi was to have been that he was dining with friends a mile away in Mayfair's swanky Clermont Club, two doors away from 42 Berkeley Square (the address of London's Number 42 Club). After also attacking his wife, who had found him with the body but escaped, he drove 42 miles to Uckfield where, in the house of a friend, he wrote at least three letters, saying in one, 'I will lie doggo for a while.' Since Newhaven, where two fishermen believed they may have seen him near the harbour, there have been only false sightings (notably resulting in the capture in Australia of a surprised John Stonehouse, the fake-suicide English MP). In 2009 *The Sun* newspaper reported that Lord Lucan was still registered as a member of the Clermont Club. If still alive, this year he would be marking 37 years on the run and his 77th birthday.

Dodi Fayed

Because of allegations of conspiracy to murder, a criminal investigation was conducted by the UK police into the deaths of Diana, Princess of Wales (36) and her companion Dodi Fayed (42) who were killed in a Paris car crash in 1997 while being chased by *paparazzi*. The investigation lasted three years and concluded that there had not been a conspiracy. A coroner's inquest in London returned a verdict, ten years after their deaths, that Diana and Dodi were unlawfully killed as a result of 'gross negligence' by the driver, Henri Paul and the *paparazzi*. Hours after the crash a security guard, Le Van Than, had sprayed red a white Fiat Uno of the same year and colour as a vehicle that had been in collision with the rear wing of Diana and Dod's rented Mercedes. Le Van Than and a *paparazzo*, Langevin, known by Henri Paul, refused requests to give evidence at the inquest.

Alumni of the Forty-Two Gang

The Forty-Two Gang started around 1925 in Chicago's Little Italy. The gang members comprised boys, teenagers and young men who committed crimes including theft and burglary. A possibly true story has the reason for the name down to a wish to be one better than Ali Baba and the Forty Thieves although, of course, Ali Baba was distinctly not allied with the 40 thieves.

Alumni of the gang and their subsequent spheres of nefarious influence include 'Milwaukee Phil' Alderiso* (Milwaukee), 'The Typewriter' Nicoletti * (Chicago), 'The

---

* In 1962, two years before the release of Bond film Goldfinger, Alderiso and Nicoletti were questioned by police while waiting in a car pimped with switches to independently control the head and tail lights—just conceivably advantageous if your battery was on the fritz—and a substantial secret cubby hole with racking sufficient for a minor arsenal. They said they were waiting for a friend.

Waiter' Ricca (Chicago), 'Diamond Joe' Esposito (Chicago), 'Mad Sam' DeStefano (Chicago), 'Willie Potatoes' (Chicago), Marcello Caifano (Las Vegas), 'Skids' Caruso (Chicago) and Sam Giancana (Chicago), 'Cock-eyed' Fratto (Des Moines), 'Teets' Battaglia (Chicago)—the latter supposedly being the first of the 42 gang to join the Capone Gang and who, after Ricca, emulated Al Capone as boss of the powerful Chicago Outfit.

Gang leader Sam Giancana had a mistress, Judith Exner, who had been introduced to President Kennedy, when he was 42, by another of her lovers, Frank Sinatra. Reputedly she became one of JFK's lovers, later giving varying accounts of her relationships. In one she said that the President requested her to contact Sam Giancana with a view to arranging for the assassination of Fidel Castro and a book by the Cuban intelligence chief, Fabian Escalante called *Executive Action: 638 Ways to Kill Fidel Castro*, lists the many CIA anti-Castro plots he estimates were detected. Demarcated by presidency, 42 of these were during the time of the Kennedy White House.

In 2007 the existence of a formal link between the CIA and the mafia departed from the flaky conspiracy theory zone with the publication of a US government report known as the 'Family Jewels'. Along with much else the report confirmed Sam Giancana's role (in the guise of 'Sam Gold') in accessing two disaffected Cubans willing to attempt to poison Castro's comestibles. The CIA then dispensed six poisonous pills, effectively bearing Fidel's name, to characters it circuitously described as 'assets that may assist in a sensitive mission requiring gangster-type action'. Completing the final leg of the poison's journey was more difficult, and that particular plan was said to have been abandoned after the substantial failure of an invasion of Cuba which included two CIA agents, Grayston Lynch and 'Rip' Robertson, at Girón Beach near the Bay of Pigs shortly into the new dawn of the Kennedy administration.

Sam Giancana died a violent death in 1975 at the age of 67 being shot in the back of the head while frying sausages in the kitchen. He was due to have been an FBI witness in an investigation into organised crime. A police guard had been called away from his home.

James Earl Ray meets Mad Frankie Fraser

Mad Frankie Fraser is a London gangster, even as an octogenarian he continues to trade on his notoriety into which is incorporated a claimed 42 years in prison. He has a website, madfrankiefraser.co.uk, where there are pictures of Mr Fraser speaking at the prestigious Oxford Union, online offers to sell branded T-shirts, mentions of his personally guided tours of London's gangland, and a curious link to a micro-site with the address of www.costadelkrays.info on which there appears an apartment for sale on Spain's Costa del Sol. There are various tales, and one is of the improbable but true assemblage of four of the most notorious criminals of the 20th century.

The time was the spring of 1968, Louis Armstrong's *What a Wonderful World** had been at the top of the charts for four weeks, and then transistor radios in England began to deliver some startling opening chords from the guitar of Keith Richards as he played a new tune called *Jumpin' Jack Flash*. Bobby Charlton and Manchester United beat Eusebio

* Aficionados will know this was the song chosen by Douglas Adams to end the original radio series of *The Hitch-hiker's Guide to the Galaxy*

and Benfica bringing the European Cup to England. In the top security wing of London's Brixton prison Mad Frankie Fraser was serving two sentences for violent crime when the Kray twins were suddenly arrested for murder and imprisoned in the same unit. The three UK criminals were joined by a US citizen, James Earl Ray, who sixty four days earlier had shot and killed the American civil rights leader, Dr Martin Luther King.

The imprisonment of James Earl Ray had been the result of extensive, determined and effective police effort. Ray had been convicted twice for armed robbery, escaped from jail, and evaded capture for a year. In preparing to kill Martin Luther King and escape detection the killer deployed four aliases: Harold Lowmeyer bought the rifle; Eric Galt—driving a white Mustang—booked a Memphis hotel room the previous night; John Willard then checked into Bessie Brewer's Rooming House, specifying a room that happened to be facing the Lorraine Motel; Paul Bridgeman stayed at a Toronto boarding house and Ramon Sneyd acquired a Canadian passport in the name of a Toronto policeman and then departed North America for Europe.

James Earl Ray could quite conceivably have escaped detection but immediately after the fatal shot he appeared to have panicked. As he left the rooming house someone remarked to him about hearing a gunshot and then in flight to his car he dropped the rifle, wrapped in only a blanket and bearing his fingerprints. A white Mustang, later also found with his fingerprints, was seen driving away.

The car was found in Atlanta and questioning about Galt in Birmingham revealed that he liked dancing and that the car had been in Los Angeles. A picture of Galt was found at an LA dance studio. It was decided to check Galt's fingerprints against fugitives and the identity of escapee James Earl Ray as the murderer was established. Cellmates of Ray told both of possible bounties that had been offered if Martin Luther King was killed and that Ray had said when he escaped from prison he was heading to Canada as it was easy to get a passport in the name of a Canadian citizen.

The Canadians compared Ray's photograph with 175,000 passport applications and on June 1st told the FBI that their suspect matched the application of George Sneyd, who had already flown to London on May 5. From there he had travelled to Portugal where he replaced his original Canadian passport with another in the same name and returned to London. Now on the watch list, he was shadowed after arriving from Portugal and had stayed in the transit lounge where he would not normally have been subjected to a passport check, to wait for a flight to Belgium. He was arrested on June 8th and was found to be carrying a handgun.

James Earl Ray was extradited and pleaded guilty without a trial to receive a 99 year sentence rather than the death penalty, then immediately began a campaign for a trial, which reached the US Supreme Court, but was unsuccessful. He died in prison in 1998 from Hepatitis C liver failure.

During the time together in Brixton Prison Mad Frankie Fraser said that James Earl Ray had told him he was innocent. Since then questions regarding James Earl Ray's motive, the possibility of his being involved in a conspiracy, and his guilt or innocence have been asked. The House Select Committee on Assassinations reported in 1978 that Ray was responsible and that there was a likelihood of a conspiracy.

CK

In 1969 Charles Kray (42) was tried alongside his brothers—the infamous Kray Twins—in London's Old Bailey and sentenced to ten years jail for aiding his siblings in disposing of a body. Ronnie and Reggie received life sentences for murder but Charles denied being involved up until his death in prison thirty years later; he had been imprisoned again after being convicted of supplying cocaine to undercover police officers.

The Birdless Man of Alcatraz

Cell 42 on Alcatraz Island was once the home of Robert Stroud who wasn't permitted any avian companions in Alcatraz on being transferred to 'The Rock' in 1942. After murdering a guard he spent 42 years in solitary confinement in different prisons. Alcatraz can be reached by ferry from San Francisco's pier…33.

The Crime of The Century

The British Great Train Robbery took place on August 8th 1963. Over £2.6 million worth of used banknotes being returned to the Bank of England for pulping were stolen*. The Bank of England's online inflation calculator shows that the amount stolen is the equivalent of £42 million in 2011; the theft was then the largest in British history with *The New York Times* determining that it was the 'Crime of the Century'.

Despite having bought an isolated farmhouse in which to hide, their unusual presence was noted by an alert bucolic while checking his livestock. Open-to-air police communications alerted the gang that their location would suddenly become less than felicitous and the rushed nature of their departure meant that they had left their fingerprints, including some found on the Monopoly game being used

---

* The locomotive, numbered 40126, was infamous amongst rail crew, having had four serious incidents occurring in four succeeding years. As well as the Great Train Robbery, she had collided with another train a few months earlier, killing eighteen. In 1964 a crewman had been electrocuted while standing on her and the same year she had been diverted onto another line just in time when the brakes failed approaching the main station in Birmingham. Eventually scrapped in 1982, the National Railway Museum in Yorkshire had turned down the chance to preserve a phenomenal tourist attraction.

to play for real money. Their board is displayed at the Sulhamstead police training centre.

The great train robbers proved not quite so great on getaways, with 12 of the believed 15 associates being caught and convicted. Those caught first received prison sentences of up to 30 years, many at the time considered this be overly harsh—those caught later getting ten years.

The gang's leader had been Bruce 'Napoleon' Reynolds who had been caught only after returning, with his wife and son, to Britain from Mexico and renting a pleasing villa in docile Torquay. Said to have been dobbed-in by his milkman for paying the bill in fivers this is probably not true, and Reynolds certainly believed otherwise, having already had a 'close shave' in London he had visited again, returning with a case of champagne. It seems more believable that he had pushed his luck too far, been recognised, and followed back to Devon.

The most famous train robber, Ronnie Biggs, received 30 years. In popular mythology he played the most minor of roles, supposedly only recruiting a mysterious 'Stan Agate' to shunt the train. (A real Stan Agate existed as the successful racing tipster of the *News of the World.*) Biggs's man was supposedly unable to operate the Class 40 locomotive... thereby leading the gang to use violence on the driver of the train. The police never appeared to seek the 'Stan Agate' gang member.

Ronnie Biggs was helped to escape from Wandsworth Prison a little over a year into his sentence. A rope ladder was thrown over the wall and other prisoners held back warders while the great train robber effected his egress. After hiding in Australia he moved to Brazil in 1970 and stayed there, for most of the time openly, until 2001 when his health deteriorated and he returned to England in declining health to spend a further eight years in prison before being released on compassionate grounds in 2009. The great train robbery had taken place on his 34th birthday.

A letter is displayed on Mad Frankie Fraser's interweb site purporting to be from a solicitor representing one of the prisoners who had helped impede guards while Biggs climbed the rope ladder over the prison wall. The letter is addressed to the sister of Mad Frankie Fraser and states that the assisting convict had authorised his brief to hold money rewarding his client for assisting in the escape of Ronnie Biggs.

Stolen Carbon

The Graff jewellery retailer in London has been subjected to six armed robberies resulting in the loss of around £84m between 1980 and 2009. In Graff I the 45 carat Marlborough diamond was stolen by thieves caught as they arrived back at Chicago O'Hare airport but the diamond has never been seen again. Graff III (£23m in 2003) and Graff VI (£40m in 2009) occurred in the same Mayfair shop, each being the biggest jewellery raids in the UK at the time. In Graff VI a diamond necklace worth up to £3.5 million and 42 other pieces comprising 1437 diamonds worth up to £37 million were stolen although for insurance purposes the jewels were valued at £26m—and of this amount Graff was reported to have lost £6.6m as their full value was not covered by their insurance deal. Two Serbians were convicted in the Graff trial and four Londoners were convicted of being involved in Graff VI. Most of the jewels stolen including the bulk of Graf III and all of Graff VI have never been recovered.

Roman Polanski

The film director was released from prison after serving 42 days of an in-prison psychiatric evaluation having entered into a plea bargain on six charges by pleading guilty to one of unlawful sexual intercourse, committed with a 13 year old at the home of Jack Nicholson whom he knew was on a skiing trip although his victim had understood she was going there to meet him. Four days after his release and before sentencing he fled from the United States and has lived mainly in France where, as a French citizen, he cannot be extradited. As he was never sentenced all six charges are still pending against him in the US.

At the request of US authorities in 2009 he was taken into Swiss custody at Zurich airport as he travelled to accept a lifetime achievement award at the Zurich film festival. After being granted house arrest he was released from that requirement in 2010 when the Swiss Justice Minister denied the US extradition request on the grounds that full testimony regarding the original sentencing requirement had not been produced, meaning that it was possible for the 42 day psychiatric assessment to have been intended to constitute a suitable sentence for unlawful sex with a 13 year old—which he had therefore already served.

Timeshare trial

In 2004 the BBC published an Underworld Rich List naming or alluding to the identities of 30 individuals or groups in the UK whose assets had come from crime. Heading the BBC's list was John Palmer, with an estimated wealth of around £300 million. In a surprising one-off interview with Elizabeth Nash for *The Independent* newspaper in 1999 during the course of which the journalist was reproved for having the temerity to look around while in his Tenerife office (vast, with a marble-floor, a marble fountain, a tank of tropical fish and a collection of carriage clocks) John Palmer claimed that the timeshare fraud charges were a result of the Brinks-Mat 'affair' in which three tonnes of gold were stolen from a Brinks-Mat secure facility at Heathrow airport in 1983, melted down and sold. *The Independent* article stated that he had paid £360,000 to settle a civil action brought by Lloyds insurers relating to the Brinks-Mat gold and believed that the timeshare fraud charges at the Old Bailey Courts in London, relating to the years between 1991 and 1995 during which he turned forty-two, were being trumped-up by the police as a consequence and were silly—a few complaints being understandable from 100,000 timeshare owners.

John Palmer told Elizabeth Nash he wouldn't be sent down and wasn't worried about anything—but unconvincingly jibbed on a request for some timeshare sales literature she could take away with her. In the event, a little under two years later at the Old Bailey, he was convicted of fraud involving 16,000 people who had signed timeshare contracts. After his conviction Mr Palmer stayed in prison in the UK for four years after which he was arrested when entering Spain by the Spanish police and imprisoned in a high-security jail for two years without being charged, eventually being released on bail. At the same time group civil actions were being pursued to recover some of the defrauded losses.

The Moorgate Control

A Moorgate Control is a system fitted to London underground trains to automatically apply the brakes if the train were to pass through a terminal station towards a blanked-off tunnel wall. These were fitted as a consequence of the mystery following the Moorgate disaster of 1975 in which 42 passengers died at the scene and around 70 more were injured when the driver continued through Moorgate Station, even appearing to accelerate, before smashing into the tunnel end at 40 mph. No cause was ever proved; the driver, Leslie Newson, was shown to have been holding down the dead man's handle at the moment of collision.

First Class Passenger Syndrome

The Corner was approaching fast and Captain Edward Smith was on the horns of a dilemma. It was Sunday evening, darkness was near, and he had to make a decision. Under normal conditions America-bound ships reaching the 42nd parallel, having avoided the known iceberg areas off Newfoundland, turned the wheel to starboard at 'The Corner' to make a direct route over the remaining 1350 miles of their transatlantic journey to New York.

The first component of his dilemma was that captains of eastbound ships, including vessels even further south near the 41st parallel, had been radioing with sightings of icebergs which could be directly in his path. To avoid them would mean steaming further south before making his turn or resting up for the night to wait for light or, a third option, slowing down to proceed with greater caution. The second part of the dilemma was called First Class Passenger Syndrome. Aboard was his 'Line' manager, Mr J. Bruce Ismay, the chairman of the White Star line and the son of 'Baccy' Ismay the self-made founder of the line which had been merged into J. Pierpoint Morgan's massive International Mercantile Marine. (Morgan had been due to sail with the *Titanic* but late in the day decided to stay on in Europe.) Ismay and Smith knew that by maintaining speed the Titanic could make a triumphant maiden arrival in New York (where IMM had just opened a palatial new office building) on Tuesday evening rather than Wednesday morning. Seemingly inconsequential in comparison with jet travel, an earlier berthing for the new liner would win lead stories in the newspapers and help sell tickets in the competition with Cunard's RMS *Mauretania* which was regarded as an 'ocean greyhound' and held the Blue Riband having made the speediest combined eastbound and westbound Atlantic crossings. (Like a boy-racer with twin chromed exhausts the *Titanic* had a dummy fourth funnel to make it appear to be as virile as the popular four-funnelled Cunard liners.)

Any time spent going south beyond The Corner reduced the chance of reaching New York on Tuesday. Ismay and Smith were overheard during the afternoon while casually sat in a public lounge discussing the ship's performance so far and planning a trial to discover her top speed the following day. Both were totally aware of the iceberg warnings. Ismay had even read one to a group of passengers. How much Ismay influenced Captain Smith's fateful decision will never be known but the outcome could be viewed as a wishful compromise. The sea was calm, visibility was excellent and sailing conditions were perfect apart from two things; there were icebergs ahead and there was no moon—which made it impossible to see an iceberg unless it was very close. Smith didn't turn at The Corner but the delay was for less than hour which placed the ship and her passengers only about 15 miles further south, perhaps hoping he would cut below the iceberg field. Fatefully, there was absolutely no lessening of speed.

The known risk meant that lookouts were instructed to be vigilant and Captain Smith stayed close to the bridge but even when lookouts believed they had seen icebergs passing to the side, where the ship's lights may have lit them up, there was still no reduction in speed. The final warning of 'Iceberg, right ahead!' came only a very few seconds before striking it. RMS *Titanic* was steaming at 42 kilometres an hour when she struck the iceberg.

The northern route was closed on news of the disaster but not before another ship, the *Rhein,* had sailed through the location of the *Titanic*'s disaster. Mrs Henry Buell, a passenger, recounted seeing some of the bodies and flotsam—thoughtfully noting the 23 icebergs of varying dimensions that surrounded the *Rhein*.

Captain Smith went down with his ship, it was to have been his final voyage before retirement. Bruce Ismay survived but was vilified in the newspapers for having taken a place on a lifeboat while there were still women and children on board and was forced from public life. As a direct result of the disaster and within three years J. Pierpoint Morgan's commercial colossus, IMM, had to ask for bankruptcy protection.

A Myth

There is a myth on the interweb that the *Titanic* should have carried 42 lifeboats rather than the 20 that were available. The true story is that the first drawings for the ship showed capacity for 64 lifeboats but this number was reduced to 48 by senior management at the White Star Line. Even this capacity wasn't filled as there was a convenient belief that lifeboats were surplus to requirements on a vessel that wasn't going to sink and if it were in trouble would stay afloat long enough for help to arrive. Lifeboats took up premium space on the promenade deck. The twenty on board was just over the legal minimum for ships over 10,000 tons even though the *Titanic* was 46,000 tons. The shortfall in lifeboats was 'compensated' by an over-supply of 3,560 life-vests which were useless in cold North Atlantic water. One of the surviving life-vests with signatures of those who escaped in lifeboat 1 was auctioned for £60,000 in 2008.

42 Lifeboats

Occurrences occurred when the London-born ship's captain, Henry Kendall, passed a landmark known as Pointe-au-Père on the St Lawrence River in Canada. The first notable event resulted in a synchronised climax of activity amongst the world's headline writers when Captain Kendall's ship, having crossed the Atlantic, neared Pointe-au-Père on a sunny Sunday morning in July 1910. Anyone on board watching their Captain might have seen that he seemed to be keeping a close watch on another passenger, a Mr Robinson, who was stood at the rail watching as four pilots boarded, having approached from the pilot's station at Pointe-au-Père. The pilots were watching their footing as they ascended the side of the ship.

Captain Kendall, his first officer, his Marconi radio operator, and the whole of the world's newspaper-reading public knew what Mr Robinson didn't: the four pilots were British and Canadian police officers in disguise and their leader was an Inspector Walter Dew of the London police. The Inspector spoke briefly with the Captain before sharing the secret with Mr Robinson. Dispensing with 'Welcome to Canada' and generic weather-based chit-chat Inspector Dew just said, 'Crippen, I want you.'

One of the most widely reported crimes of the century Dr Crippen poisoned his wife with scopolamine, hid her body, partly in the basement, and fled with his lover, correctly believing that the police suspected him. His plan was for them both to head back to his native USA as a Mr Robinson and a Master Robinson. Despite boarding in Antwerp, Captain Kendall had soon suspected them of matching a police description he had been given, seeing the 'boy' squeeze his father's hand in a manner familiar rather than filial. Before losing contact with Marconi's Cornish radio station at Poldhu, Captain Kendall sent an 'ethergram' alerting the police who promptly boarded a faster ship. This overtook the *Montrose* allowing them to await the Robinsons. The story of the anticipated arrest of the suspected London cellar murderer was front page headlines around the world. Dr Crippen was brought back to London, tried, and hung within four months.

Captain Kendall's triumph turned into tragedy of the worst kind in four years and just a few miles from Pointe-au-Père. A new command, the prestigious RMS *Empress of*

Ireland, was a fast ship able to ferry mail, passengers and cargo between Quebec and Liverpool in six days. In the early hours of May 29th 1914, the *Empress*, having dropped off the pilot at Pointe-au-Père, needed to cross back over to the other side of the river. Captain Kendall saw the lights of a Norwegian coal-carrier, SS *Storstad*, approaching but believed it was safe to cross its path. Visibility was suddenly lost in a fog bank and he ordered the engines to stop. The reinforced ice-breaking bow of the SS *Storstad* then re-appeared 30 metres away to ram the *Empress* directly amidships.

The collision was absolutely catastrophic. The *Empress of Ireland* immediately listed hard over to starboard submerging within 14 minutes. It was the worst disaster in Canadian maritime history; there had been 42 lifeboats on board but there hadn't been time to launch any more than a handful. 1024 died including 840 passengers—eight more than had perished on the *Titanic*. Only 42 of the survivors were women, a much smaller proportion than had survived the *Titanic*. All except four of 138 children died. Of the 420 crew, 184 died and 236 survived. Shown by a white buoy, the wreck of the *Empress of Ireland* lies eight miles off Pointe-au-Père, in 42 metres of water.

The Universe

A Long History of Telescopes

Pursuing the finest possible telescope has been a predilection of astronomers for over 400 years, competition to have the best being a defining constant. Sagittarians (22 November—22 December) and Librans (24 September—23 October) are especially hot on ogling optics. A simple guide to the story can be constructed from four instruments linked by ten-fold leaps in the key measure of the diameter of the light-gathering power.

Diameter	Year	Main Optic	Telescope
4.2 centimetres (nearly)	1620	Lens	A very early model made soon after the first telescope. This one was one of Galileo's *Perspicilli*. Easily portable
42 centimetres (almost)	1847	One large lens	Harvard University's *Harvard Great Refractor* Making perfect large lenses was and still is technically a very tricky proposition indeed. This one was the largest telescope in the USA for 20 years. In Europe there were already considerably larger mirror-technology telescopes
4.2 metres	1987	One quite big mirror	UK-Netherlands *William Herschel Telescope*, Canary Islands
42 metres	Planned for 2018	Five big mirrors	The European ELT—Extremely Large Telescope, Chile

Boldly going beyond 'very' and 'extremely' in the telescope name one-upmanship game is a plan published by the European Space Organisation for a 100m diameter telescope very amusingly named OWL: the Overwhelmingly Large Telescope.

Seeing the World In A Grape

Smart thinking doesn't only happen on ergonomically-borne buttocks in a status corner office with a designer desk and hot PA. At the outbreak of the First World War the physicist and professor Karl Schwarzchild immediately stepped up to enlist in the German Army and fight for his country. In 1915 as Einstein published the paper containing his general theory of relativity Schwarzchild was on the Russian front, a place of horrendous conflict, but within weeks he was first to divine the exact solution to the Einstein field equations of general relativity.

His work included identifying the eponymous Schwarzchild radius. This predicted the possibility of black holes—any object with mass becoming smaller than its Schwarzchild radius will continue collapsing under its own gravity. This applies to the Earth. The size at which we would all be living inside our own personal black hole occurs the instant the Earth's diameter drops to less than 18 millimetres—a planet the size of a svelte grape.

Not long after this triumph Karl Schwarzchild developed a quite horrible autoimmune skin condition which, pre-antibiotics, commonly lead to serious secondary infections. Having solved Einstein's field equations on the battlefield, he died there, aged 42.

Expanding Universe Scientists

Belonging to the European Organisation for Nuclear Research near Geneva, the Large Hadron Collider is a 27 kilometre tube capable of making small bits of things very dizzy, crashing them, and seeing what flew off. The idea is to try and understand more about life, the universe and everything. When the expanding number of LHC scientists acquired more office accommodation recently they named their new complex Building 42.

Multiple experiments use the LHC. One of these is FP420

looking at the feasibility of additional detectors placed 420m away from the main collision area. A spokesman on this project was the erudite Lancastrian and TV presenter, Professor Brian Cox, who was 'chuffed' to be given an OBE at 42 in the Queen's 2010 Birthday Honours.

Astronomy Precinct

Astronomy Precinct, beside the summit of Mauna Kea on Hawaii, is probably the finest star-gazing real estate in the world. At 4,200m the elevation puts you effortlessly (Steve, a personable Iowan with a driving licence drove our micro-coach) above some 42% of the earth's atmosphere. Regularly clear skies and the smooth, cool wind means that the 'astronomical seeing' is expressed as around 0.42 arcseconds or...twinkless, twinkless little stars.

The superior seeing has made Astronomy Precinct home to the world's finest collection of a kind of time machine—telescopes detecting scintilla of light that started their trip to Astronomy Precinct billions of years earlier. The dozen fantastic instruments include the giant Pair of Kecks, funded by well-trousered philanthropist W.M.

Keck; Japan's massive Subaru (昴) the largest single mirror telescope in the world (not named as I supposed after the automobile manufacturer but more romantically for the *Pleiades,* or Seven Sisters, star cluster, which you may make out even in daylight by standing in front of any Subaru); and the James Clerk Maxwell, notable to lovers of anoraks for both possessing the world's largest piece of Gore-Tex®, and for making the first earthly observation of the afterglow of GRB 090423, a massive explosion indicating the formation of a black hole. It is the most distant and hence oldest object ever seen having occurred when the universe was 630 million years old, a nudge over 4.2% of the present age.

Escape Velocity

A speed of 42 kilometres per second is needed to escape from the phenomenon known as the sun's gravity if starting from somewhere on earth.

This is 35 times faster than the fastest rifle bullet—yet supermacho quantum physicists think of gravity as such a weakling force they are quite happy to ignore it.

They Could be Twins

Name on passport	M42	M42
Known to her mates as…	Périphérique de Birmingham	The Orion Nebula
In a nutshell for Guardian readers, what is it?	Popular six lane cut-through between Catshill in Worcestershire (population 4428) and Appleby Magna in Leicestershire (population 1050). Carries 120,000 vehicles a day	A lot of dust (think bag-less vacuum cleaner) plus brown dwarfs plus proto-planets. So vast, its own gravity makes new stars. Currently our nearest spot to go and see new stars being made
And 'M' must be code for something interesting or mysterious?	An IJD (ironic joke device) left by the retreating Romans. M comes from a latin verb, *Moto,* that used to mean setting in motion	The 18th century French astronomer Charles Messier numbered 110 distractions interfering with the serious business of comet-hunting. His distractions are some of the most spectacular sights in the universe

Name on passport	**M42**	**M42**
I'm warming to this, where should I be looking?	South of Birmingham, east of Solihull. Can't miss it mate	Look for a fuzzy star in Orion's sword. NB If you are reading this by torchlight in Australia or New Zealand, remember, our Orion is your Shopping Trolley. Hey, if you're keen, why not join a Messier marathon and try to see all 110 in one wild night?
Where can I go to have a pee, ask if you've seen the astronomical price of meals in here, flock around with others in the manner favoured by decapitated poultry, and then buy a Ginsters?	Tamworth or Hopton Park	Subject to planning consent and the formation of a suitable star and planet the 42nd branch of Milliways, Douglas Adams' growing restaurant chain-cum-service station at the end of the universe. See you instore
But practically—what if the Earth were the size of a grain of sand on Blackpool Beach?	If the Earth were a grain of sand the M42 wouldn't quite get you all the way across a red blood cell	If the Earth were a grain of sand the Orion Nebula would be the size of the Earth, pre-shrinkage obviously
Speed cameras?	Yes	No

Hollywood Signs

Mr Simpson's Dark Secret

Mr Homer Simpson is not 42. Fox made an episode called 'Summer of 4 Ft. 2' being a parody of the coming-of-age film *Summer of '42* but that is not relevant. The Family Simpson enjoy a 'floating timeline'—a euphemism used to avoid the distress and all-round unpleasantness involved in having to break the news that they stay the same age while the audience gets old and dies. Mr Simpson's age has been stationed in a zone between 35 and 40. But... two birthdates have been seen. An episode first aired in 1990 shows an insurance form in which Mr Simpson's birthdate is shown as May 10th 1955, the exact same day as John Lennon's killer, Mark Chapman. This may of course have been a complete coincidence.

This would have made Mr Simpson's 42nd birthday May 10th 1997, the same day as Mark Chapman obviously, when Mr Simpson was something over a year younger than his creator Matt Groening, who was forty-three at the time. The second birth date to appear was on a driving licence seen in 1993 that showed a birthdate of May 12th 1956 with Mr Simpson sharing a first day on Earth with Kix Brooks the country music singer and songwriter, which may of course be a complete coincidence. The Yankees-Indians baseball playoff prevented Mr Simpson's 42nd birthday—counting from his first birth—being the first airdate for the episode '*The Simpson's Spin-off Showcase*' which was held over to the following day. This episode happens to have the production code 4F20 so that, I think, is a wrap.

P. Sherman, 42 Wallaby Way, Sydney

Contending for the most famous 42 in the world is part of the name and address read by Dory on a mislaid diver's mask in Disney's *Finding Nemo*. 'P Sherman, 42 Wallaby Way, Sydney' is a catchphrase in the film and the title of a song in the soundtrack. *Finding Nemo* won the animated film Oscar in 2003 and has been reported as the all-time best-selling DVD and has the highest gross sales for a g-rated—children's—film.

Quad Wranglers

A classic film scene is the climax of *Chariots of Fire* that features an attempt to race around the central quad of Cambridge's Trinity College before the clock chimes twenty-four times—at noon. The scene is based on the real Great Court Run which has only been done successfully twice; firstly in 1927 by Lord Burghley, and then in 2007 by Sam Dobin in a faster time of 42.77 seconds.

Timewarping—Again and Again and Again

Always to hand on my desk is the one book I don't keep in the toilet; Phil Farrand's *The Nitpicker's Guide for Classic Trekkers.* She's getting a little battered now but will always repay close study. For example, if you turn to page 171 it shows that the 42nd episode of *Star Trek* was called *Obsession* and was first aired on earthdate December 15th 1967, stardate 3620.7. Now, thumb through to page 179 and you see that the 42nd episode to be filmed was *The Trouble With Tribbles* which went out two weeks later on earthdate December 29th 1967 or stardate 4523.3. But thinking logically, i.e. as seen from the bridge of the USS *Enterprise*, the real 42nd episode was the 42nd episode in stardate order, which is *Mirror, Mirror* (stardate circa 3585.5, and aired on October 6th 1967). The 42nd episode of *Star Trek*: so good they made it a mind-warping three times. Thankfully all stardates in the second series of *Star Trek The Next Generation* start with 42.

I am unable to leave this most fascinating of subjects without telling you about the world's only monument to something that won't happen in the future. If you walk behind the barber's shop in the very small Iowan town of Riverside (population 928, motto 'Where the trek begins'), there is a plaque marking the official location of Captain Kirk's future birth on the March 22nd 2228. If you are following the 42nd parallel trail, it is a short but eminently worthwhile 36-mile hike to the south.

'10'

Blake Edwards' 1979 film *'10'* starring Dudley Moore, Bo Derek, beaded corn row hair, Julie Andrews, Ravel's *Bolero*, and sex, begins with Dudley Moore's character, a music writer called George Webber, celebrating his 42nd birthday.

Gung Ho

The phrase *gung ho* entered Western vocabulary after the 1942 marine raid on the Japanese soldiers holding Makin Island (now Butariti). *Gung ho's* meaning as originally intended by Evans Carlson, the raid leader, was to be working for the other fellow knowing that help would be received in turn. The raid on Makin Island was the first ever to land a force of Marine Raiders from a submarine and the raid featured in a 1943 morale-lifting war film *Gung Ho!*.

A modern 41,000 ton amphibious assault craft, the USS *Makin Island*, is currently named for the Marine Raiders who landed on the atoll. Few people knew until long after that nine marines had accidentally been left stranded on Makin Island and were beheaded by the Japanese. The fate of the nine marines was written about by Tripp Wiles in his 2007 book, *Forgotten Raiders of '42*.

And The Oscar Refusals Are…

Woody Allen has (with one exception) declined his invitation to attend the Oscar ceremony or acknowledge his three Oscars and many nominations. The first time was the 1978 Awards when his *Annie Hall* (1977) won four awards for the 42-year-old including Best Picture—ahead of *Star Wars*, and Best Director—beating both *Star Wars* and *Close Encounters of the Third Kind*. He did show once, unannounced, to support New York at the 2002 ceremony immediately following the 9/11 attack.

Three people have refused to accept their Oscar:

Dudley Nichols—*The Informer* (1935), Screenplay. Didn't attend or accept his Oscar at an awards ceremony that was boycotted as part of the Screen Writers' Guild's eight year struggle to be recognised by Hollywood producers.

George C. Scott—*Patton* (1970), Best Actor. Didn't attend, didn't accept the Oscar, later chose to call the awards event 'a meat parade'.

Marlon Brando—*The Godfather* (1972), Best Actor. Didn't attend in support of American Indian rights—sent Sacheen Littlefeather in his place.

In 2003 the Academy awarded an Oscar to an absent child rapist, Roman Polanski, allowing him to continue to avoid justice. Many of the Hollywood 'great' and 'good' stood up and applauded. Moral fog as well as smog out there.

*****Bonus trivium***** *Midnight Cowboy* (1969) starring Dustin Hoffman as Ratso and Jon Voight as Joe Buck won the Best Film Oscar in the 42nd Academy Awards having been directed by the English director John Schlesinger when he was 42. *Midnight Cowboy* was the only X-classified film ever to be shown to the President (Nixon), and is the only X-movie to ever win an Oscar.

Tomorrow, and Tomorrow, and Groundhog Day

Each morning my travels in dreamtime end in the same way. Like this:

[A bedroom in a Shropshire home]

THE VOICE	It is 6.29 am and the in-mates are asleep.
F/X	DISPLAY ON THE RADIO ALARM ROLLS ONTO 6.30 am.
GRAMS	MUSIC: *Ding-ding...Ding-ding...Ding-diding...DING...*

And it's time to start another day to the sound of—just in case you haven't guessed—Sonny & Cher's original of *I Got You Babe*. I love *Groundhog Day* and try to watch it every day. For readers who have been holding out on a jungle island, firstly, well done, and secondly this is the film in which a TV reporter played by Bill Murray (forty-two) is covering a perennial story about a weather-predicting marmot, expertly played by method groundhog Punxsatawney Phil (of unknown age but definitely old). If Punxsy Phil, who resides in Gobbler's Knob (where else?), should see his own shadow on Groundhog Day the United States will have 42 more days of winter. The next day Bill Murray's character wakes again to the sound of *I Got You Babe* just like the day before, and the same twenty-four hours of life starts to replay. Each morning my travels in dreamtime...

The *Groundhog Day* screenplay was written by Danny Rubin and high level concept stuff behind the movie resonates with the philosophical notion called 'eternal recurrence' which was explored in 1882 by theothanatologist Friedrich 'God is Dead' Nietzsche. Eternal recurrence cropped up again in the German philosopher's most important work, *Thus Spoke Zarathusa*, written when he was forty-two and echoing ideas found in the Greek myth of King Sisyphus. Supposedly cleverer than the god Zeus, he (Sisyphus not Nietzsche) decommissioned Death (Thanatos), then tricked his way back from hell only to be sentenced to an eternal life in which every day was to be spent pushing a boulder up a hill only to see it roll down again at day's end—a Sisyphean task. The method groundhog bit Bill Murray twice during filming.

'Nobody can eat 50 eggs'

In the classic motion picture *Cool Hand Luke*, Paul Newman's character is in prison and for a bet manages, just, to eat 50 boiled eggs in one hour. Mr Newman was 42. Here are some more ideas for egg movies.

Egg	Number of eggs eaten and the record or possible record time	Normalised to 42 eggs
Raw	13 in 1.04 seconds	0 minutes 3.4 seconds
Scrambled	30 in 45 seconds	0 minutes 35 seconds
Quail (pickled)	42 in 1 minute	1 minute 0 seconds
Soft boiled	32 in 55 seconds	1 minutes 12 seconds
Hard boiled (Sonya Thomas)	65 in 6 minutes 40 seconds	4 minutes 18 seconds
Cadbury's Creme	10 in 2 minutes 11 seconds	9 minutes 10 seconds
Pickled	3 in 58 seconds	13 minutes 32 seconds
Crocodile	10 in 4 minutes 24 seconds	18 minutes 28 seconds
Scotch	13½ in 7 minutes	21 minutes 47 seconds
Cool Hand Luke (Hard boiled)	50 in 60 minutes	50 minutes 23 seconds

Cool Hand Luke was produced by actor Jack Lemmon's production company. The record time for peeling and eating a lemon is 9.84 seconds.

*****Bonus trivium*****

It is a popular myth that Joanna Woodward, Paul Newman's wife, was star #1 on the Hollywood Walk of Fame (which is to undergo a planned $4.2m makeover). Joanna Woodward's star had been one of eight examples displayed before construction but the work was delayed for some two years until 1960 (in part because of a legal challenge by Charlie Chaplin Jr, his father, having been selected at first was omitted from the proposed inaugural installation of several hundred stars) and the first star fixed in place was that of the film producer (*High Noon*) and director (*Guess Who's Coming to Dinner*), Stanley Kramer. Charlie Chaplin finally got his star in 1972.

The Best Western

The Best Western is the world's largest hotel chain with over 4,200 hotels in 80 countries, it says here on the interweb, and it is true that I have always enjoyed a topping night and spiffing breakfast but my Best Western is *Butch Cassidy and the Sundance Kid*, so here are six bullet points about it.

- Bob Dylan, it is said, was offered the chance to sing *Raindrops Keep Fallin' on My Head*, Hal David and Burt Bacharach's song which was to receive the Best Song Oscar for that year. If so, His Bobness passed on the opportunity, but not too long afterwards could be observed appearing in *Pat Garrett and Billy the Kid*, also writing the score for the Sam Peckinpah film and slipping in a little tune called *Knockin' on Heaven's Door*—quite easily worth two Oscars yet not winning one, not even a nomination. I do believe The Academy should be sent to stand in their own naughty corner for that one. And if it doesn't have one, they should award itself One.

- The time spent by the real Butch and Sundance in Argentina after buying a ranch in the Cholila Valley, now a 'cowboy and fly-fishing dreamland', is part of *In Patagonia*, the distinctively chaptered portmanteau English writer Bruce Chatwin based on a jaunt made after parting with some style from a job on the *Sunday Times* by despatching a telegram 'Have gone to Patagonia'.

- The film screenplay was written by William Goldman who researched his material for eight years and for which 20th Century Fox paid $400,000, which after adjusting for time is one of the most expensive original scripts in Hollywood history, the equivalent of some $5.3m today. The film won four Oscars at the 42nd Academy Awards in 1970.

- Butch Cassidy lead The Wild Bunch from two hideouts; the Hole in the Wall gang's Hole in the Wall which was in Wyoming's Big Horn Mountains, and a remote Utah canyon now in Canyonlands National Park called Robbers' Roost. In 2003 Aron Ralston, an experienced walker and climber, was exploring a narrow slot canyon in Robbers' Roost when he became trapped after a boulder moved, pinning his arm. After five days alone a desperate Aron used a Leatherman-type multi-tool to amputate himself from his arm—after first breaking the bones of his forearm.

- *Butch Cassidy and the Sundance Kid* lifted the already very successful careers of both Paul Newman and Robert Redford. In 1969, the year of the release of the film, Robert Redford bought land in Utah that is now the Sundance ski resort, named after his character and where he also located the Sundance Film Festival. Paul Newman founded the Association of Hole In The Wall Camps for children with serious medical conditions and co-founded Newman's Own, a substantial food corporation that donates all profits to charity.

✸ The final shoot-out may be fiction. Their last confirmed postal address was the Argentina ranch in 1907. In Bolivia, the police never knew the identity of either of the two men who had been responsible for a mine payroll robbery near Tupiza and who had died from bullet wounds. It was later conjecture by others that the two might have been Butch and Sundance. Searches to discover where the two did die have failed despite a number of exhumations in Bolivia and in the United States. If the two men in Bolivia had been Butch and Sundance, then Butch Cassidy had been forty-two when he died and the Sundance Kid had been forty-one.

Lost

42 was one of the six numbers in *Lost*. *Lost* was like *Gilligan's Island*, being partly filmed on Oahu, Hawaii.

Some of You Ain't Heard Nothing Yet

Elvis Presley of the 1910s, '20s and '30s was Al Jolson, who could with ease sell out New York's Winter Garden, and anywhere else, *before* he made the first full-length 'talkie' to then be seen and heard by the biggest every audience of the time around much of the world. The era-ending film was made in 1927 by Warner Bros.* and called *The Jazz Singer*. In truth *The Jazz Singer* wasn't much of talkie, comprising a half dozen songs with a couple of minutes of speech but this included the unbelievably apposite use of a Jolson line taken from his stage performances: 'Wait a minute, wait a minute I tell yer, you ain't heard nothing yet'. The fact was that many of the first audiences hadn't heard anything yet as their local movie theatre didn't yet possess the equipment needed to play the soundtrack, which meant that they got to see the silent version of the first talkie.

Al Jolson followed up the *The Jazz Singer* with a movie that was to be the most financially successful film with sound

* The most notable tragedy in the history of making movies was the death of Sam Warner at the age of forty. Having lead and driven development of the world's first talkie Sam Warner died of a septic sinus and ear infection the day before the première of *The Jazz Singer*—where it was immediately recognised that his idea was the future.

for the next nine years. *The Singing Fool* included the forty-two year old's new song, *Sonny Boy*—the first million-selling song originating from a movie. One of the co-writers of *Sonny Boy* was the very prolific and successful songwriter, Buddy DeSylva, who had been involved in a less fortunate collaboration with Al Jolson and another writer: all three were successfully sued for damages and future royalties by the publishers of Italian composer Giacomo Puccini after they had lifted a melody from the opera *Tosca*.

In the Second World War Al Jolson—who had been born in Lithuania—on his own initiative began a marathon journey touring and performing to US troops around the world, part-paying the cost himself. He caught malaria somewhere on the tour and had a lung removed, but five years later when the Korean War started Al Jolson called the White House and promptly flew to Korea to give 42 troop concerts—paying himself—in sixteen days. Shortly after his return from Korea the greatest entertainer of the first half of the twentieth century suffered a heart attack and died aged sixty-four.

Good Vibrations

British Summer Time (42 bpm)

In the list of the one best summer records of all time the only possible choice is *In the Summertime* (42 beats per minute) by *Mungo Jerry*. Written by the Ray Dorset from Kent with wrap-around sideburns the song was seemingly at number one for the whole of the summer of 1970 and the best-selling single in the UK that year. World sales are now estimated to be around thirty million copies.

Doubting Sigismund

There is a story about Mozart that says he composed the work called *Cantata on Christ's Grave* in 1767 by way of a test that had been set by Archbishop Sigismund of Salzburg who couldn't believe that the 11-year-old was working unaided. Sigismund issued Mozart with pen, ink and paper, the story goes, and then placed him in solitary confinement. Some days later the Archbish was listening to the world première of *GrabMusik* (Grave Music, Köchel catalogue K. 42). The piece has continued to be regularly performed but the reality is that the tale of Mozart's personal 11+ exam is likely to be a myth as details of the test would probably have been mentioned in his father's extensive writings.

Remarkably, Mozart was to produce his final work while dying at the age of only 35. It was the terminally sublime *Requiem in D minor* (K. 626) and Mozart began realising the commission was going to be for himself when after being ill for a while and complaining of being poisoned he started swelling horribly—possibly from a streptococcal infection. He died still applying the finishing touches and the great, sad, final piece was completed by friends.

Alternative Decibels

'Too many decibels!' is an increasingly commonly heard cry these days. The solution is at hand in the new deciAdams scale, which in one neat pocket-sized ten point scale from 0 to 8 covers everything from the quietest to the loudest sounds you will ever hear.

dA	dB	Sounds like
0 x 42	0dB	Hearing the sound of a mosquito 3 metres away. Perhaps interestingly the mosquito doesn't hear itself or other mosquitoes. Using an unbelievably sensitive Johnston's organ at the base of each antenna they detect the air being moved as a result of the rapidly beating wings rather than the changes in air pressure that we hear as sound. Then they have sex
1 x 42	42dB	Whispering '42 decibels' is about 42 decibels
2 x 42	84dB	The sound level in a busy restaurant and on the cusp of causing hearing loss for the very frequent diner
3 x 42	126dB	The Who performing in 1976 at Charlton's football ground. For several years this was cited as the world's loudest rock band although Mountain's bassist, Felix Pappalardi, was probably the first musician to have retired from industrial deafness caused through his own music. Pappalardi—who had notably also produced Cream—was shot dead in 1983 by his 42 year old wife

dA	dB	Sounds like
4 x 42	168dB	A cruising 747 airliner. This is the noise level outside the aircraft. The noise in the cabin varies according to how close your seat is to the proud young couple with the remarkably voluble baby
4.2 x 42	178dB	Just below the loudest car sound systems. 'dB drag racing' folk spend thousands and thousands in their attempts to gain decimals on their decibels. Instantly causes irreparable hearing damage, of course
5 x 42	210dB	One ton of TNT. Exploding obviously. Over 192dB sound energy is classified as a shockwave as it moves faster than the speed of sound in air
6 x 42	252dB	Hiroshima and Nagasaki atomic bombs
7 x 42	294dB	Earthquake of 8.6 on the Richter scale
8 x 42	336dB	This level is louder than any sound ever thought to have been heard on earth. The Tambora volcanic explosion in Indonesia in 1815 may have been 320dB. It caused Europe's 'year without a summer' leading to famines the following year. Krakatoa—west of Java—in 1883 may have been 310dB

Perfect Time

The three best-selling music albums are 42 minutes long.

#	Artist	Album	Playtime	Sales
1	Michael Jackson	*Thriller*	42' 19"	110 million
2	AC/DC	*Back in Black*	42' 11"	49 million
3	Pink Floyd	*The Dark Side of the Moon*	42' 59"	45 million

The Wrap Artistes

Producer Phil Spector made 42 takes when recording *Be My Baby* with The Ronettes (later making the group's Ronnie Bennett the first Mrs Spector). The song was number 22 in *Rolling Stone* magazine's top 500 songs and is Beach Boy Brian Wilson's favourite song.

Phil Spector is the only person other than Sir George Martin to produce an album (*Let It Be*) for The Beatles. The album recorded before that was the *White Album* featuring the song *Ob-La-Di Ob-La-Da* which had been a long 42 hours in the recording—being Paul McCartney's creative baby but very strongly not to John Lennon's taste. Within a few more months The Beatles had permanently un-grouped.

Ob-La-Di Ob-La-Da was never performed live by The Beatles, and Sir Paul McCartney waited forty-one years after its release before performing the song on stage. He first sang the words *Ob-La-Di Ob-La-Da* to an audience in Hamburg in December 2009 and the song has featured in subsequent set lists.

Not A Car Park

The English band Level 42 chose their name in recognition of The *Hitch-hiker's Guide to the Galaxy* and not as is oft-repeated after the world's tallest car-park. This isn't easy to locate. Contenders include the 20-storey robotic car storage facility at VW's plant in Wolfsburg, Germany, or an interesting interleaved 8+8 design in Nottingham, England. Anyway, later, in 1985, Terry Gilliam's film *Brazil*, has the central character Sam Lowry (played by Jonathan Pryce) living on Level 42.

Kings Croaking

The singing legend known to his many fans as 'The King' died at home aged 42. Jimmy Zámbó was a best-selling pop singer in Hungary with an, almost impossible, four octave voice. He was at the top of the charts at the time of his death in Christmas 2001. Jimmy died after apparently putting a 9mm Beretta bullet into his head.

Elvis Presley, another best-selling pop singer, was also called 'The King', also died at home, and was also 42. Elvis died after putting a medium-sized bowl of ice-cream and six biscuits (cookies) into his stomach.

And Everything

Mana

It is the 1300s. If you are carving stone into the image of an ancestor you are on Easter Island, and believe in Mana, the spirit associated with living, and dead, souls. If you are fashioning glass into the image of a deity within a stylised tree design you are in mediaeval western Europe and you believe in God. The contemporary Moai of Easter Island and Tree of Jesse Windows in Europe's churches demonstrate the best of religion in the same sense that Douglas Adams had believed that while JS Bach had been entirely wrong in his religious belief, an outcome of his error was the *Mass in B Minor* which he considered simply the finest work of genius ever created by man.

Moai are big. In comparison, Stonehenge's trilithons look fiddlin' and small. Of the 887 completed Moai the greatest approach ten metres (33 feet) in height. They are the largest stone sculptures in the world and all were made without metal tools. A giant of 21 metres, bigger than the Mount Rushmore Presidents, rests with his back attached to the rock never having been completed, the islanders possibly realising they couldn't have lifted or moved him. None taller than three metres have left the island, the smallest of these being the 42 centimetre fun-sized one in the Louvre in Paris.

The idea of the ancestral Tree of Jesse is from the bibles; there being forty two generations between Jesse and Joseph, the 'earthly father' of Jesus. The Jesse Windows, of which there are many, show this family lineage within a stylised tree's branches. Jesse is always lying on the ground at the bottom, propped on an elbow as if on the sofa but with a tree trunk curling away from the region of his trunk. Ascending branches support assorted bible characters, sometimes with the local great and good, before topping out the crown of the tree with a Mary and Jesus. Jesse Windows are invariably remarkable: so the only entirely surprising thing is that few people now know of them or appreciate their art—the earliest known English stained glass was part of a Jesse Window in York Minster, probably from around 1150. The most magnificent stained glass window in England (and you can still visit this treasure) is the Jesse Window of 1340 or thereabouts at Selby Abbey in Yorkshire.

The tree window idea had travelled from Europe; being effective as a way of impressing illiterate congregations, the thousands upon thousands of magically coloured, illuminated, irregular yet ordered, pixels telling a pictorial story that could only be appreciated—symbolically—from within the church. 1000 years or so later, Jesse Windows are still being installed. In contrast, the last Moai were being chiselled 350 years ago at the same time as nearly all the trees disappeared from Easter Island. It isn't known whether the events were connected. The end was sudden enough for perfect faces of unfinished heads to remain in the quarry wall, their eyes now gazing forever on a trickle of tourists.

Easter Islanders dropped their allegiance to tedious stone-age chiselling to favour a far more exciting birdman cult that required swimming with sharks to a craggy islet, scaling its cliffs, and swimming back again bearing the egg of a sooty tern; the winner achieving the mythic *tabu* status for his clan's religious leader, at least until it was time for the next round*. This idea had legs. Later additions, including cameras and Ant and Dec, have made the cult attractive to watching millions round the world who know new versions of it as

* Dangerous enough to cause deaths, the birdman competition and the birdman cult were 'ended' by European proselytisers in the 19th century. Breakfasting at Easter I had been desolated to find that there wasn't an Easter Egg on the whole of Easter Island and about to jam a consolatory bread roll when my host said that I might like to examine the underside. Baked into the bread in a *bas relief* was the spooky shape of the crouched birdman. Kindly and charming Oscar gave me a knowing look. Mana.

reality TV. And once every year, the television in many millions of homes will share prime front-of-sofa space with a decorated tree.

Cash Barrels

Crude oil is traded in 'barrels' of 42 gallons. A record price per barrel of $147.27 was reached on July 11th 2008. At this price, estimated 2010 North Sea oil production would be worth £93 billion and Bill Gates' fortune, as estimated by *Forbes* magazine in 2010, could buy 139 days worth. Well rich Saudi Arabia's estimated production is 8.5 million barrels a day in 2010 and at $147.27 the Microsoft founder's fortune would be gone in 42 days. But he would have plenty of oil.

Offers in the region of…£300m

How often do you wonder what a good skyscraper would set you back? Tower 42 has everything the discerning buyer could want, being a 600ft London landmark, visible from most points in the city, and very easy to make your way back to after even the most comprehensively liquid night out. If your interest lies in social climbing the tower brings an impressive *lettre de cachet* having been opened by Queen Elizabeth II in 1981 and being the tallest building in the UK for ten years. It is most definitely still A-list, making frequent movie appearances in establishing shots of London and even appearing in the BBC's TV version of *The Hitch-hiker's Guide to The Galaxy*. At the top is a 42nd floor restaurant; the non-revolving Vertigo 42. And the location enjoys supreme connectivity with red London buses displaying the number 42 passing every five minutes. The 2010 asking price of £300m ($461m) seemed low.

Eye Pods

Contrary to popular belief the London Eye does not have 42 pods. It has 32, a deficiency of ten. There have been a number of wheels with 42 pods, some wheels being more temporary than others.

A DEFICIENCY OF TEN

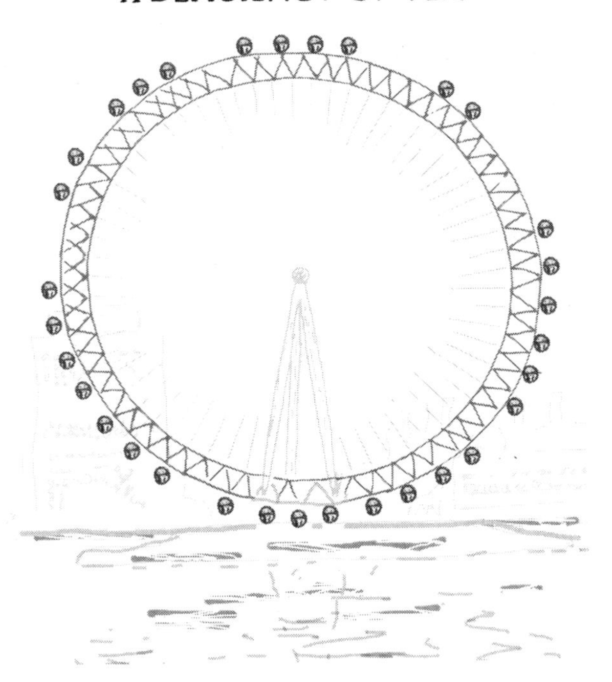

Purists seeking the full 42-pod experience should head for Manchester.

Wheel	**Location**	**Pods**
Wiener Riesenrad (featured in Graham Greene's *The Third Man*)	Vienna, Austria	15
Singapore Flyer (at 42 storeys, the world's tallest)	Singapore	28
The London Eye	UK	32
Mr Ferris's First Ferris Wheel	Chicago, USA	36
Wheel of Manchester	UK	42
Beijing Great Wheel (to be the tallest once opened)	China	48
Star of Nanchang	China	60

Six Pints of Anti-Matter (in clean glasses, please)

The highest rate of hyper-inflation was just under 42 quadrillion percent or 42,000,000,000,000,000%. This occurred in Hungary in 1946 when the price of six pints of bitter was doubling every fifteen hours. A 100,000,000,000,000,000,000 Pengo note was in circulation which was worth a few pennies in Britain. In 2008 Zimbabwe came close to matching the Hungarian rate, when their price for six pints of bitter was doubling every 25 hours.

It can be inconvenient to carry enough moolah for an evening out when inflation really sets in. A million dollars in single dollar bills weighs a metric tonne. Each bill has a thickness of one ten-thousandth of an inch more than 0.0042 inches which doesn't seem much but still stacks up very nicely: $1m in dollar bills is high enough to be able to stand on to peer over the top of St Paul's Cathedral and see what's on the other side. The most convenient means of carrying enough cash where beer is dear is the US $10,000 bill—discontinued in 1969 but still legal tender. One million dollars would then weigh 100 grams, about as little as a quarter-pounder. More than 300 of the notes exist so check your billfold for a portrait of Abraham Lincoln's Treasury Secretary, Salmon P. Chase. His rarity means that the value to a collector is about ten times face value—around $100,000 for a gram of paper.

This is very, very, very cheap compared to the costliest thing to make, which is anti-matter. Costs vary according to supplier and it pays to shop wisely. In 1999 NASA in the US estimated a cost of $62.5 trillion per anti-gram whilst in 2001 CERN in Europe quoted a price of £325 quadrillion for an anti-gram of anti-protons. This was slashed to £65 quadrillion in 2004 to try to kick-start the anti-European matter market. Whomever you select, the least convenient way of paying them would be Rai stone money from Yap Island. Their circular 'coins' resemble carved mill-stones with the largest weighing up to four tons. They are easier to carry than value, even in the past rarely having been traded for discrete goods or anti-goods. If it helps, a very small one is believed to have been worth about one good pig.

Every Picture Tells This Story

TIFF is a popular computer picture file format that belongs to Adobe. Every picture file contains the number 42 for the following reason:

> 'The second word of the file is the TIFF 'version number'. This number, 42 (2A in hex), is not to be equated with the current revision of the TIFF specification. In fact, the TIFF version number (42) has never changed, and probably never will. If it ever does, it means that TIFF has changed in some way so radical that a TIFF reader should give up immediately.
>
> *The number 42 was chosen for its deep philosophical significance.* [my italics] It can and should be used as additional verification that this is indeed a TIFF file.'

Separated After Birth

Weighing about 4200 tons if you could coax it upon the bathroom scales, a Type 42 destroyer is a warship of the British Royal Navy, and the Argentinian Armada.

Sixteen Type 42s were built between 1970 and 1983, with the first two ships having shared the same slipway for hull construction within six days of each other at Barrow-in-Furness shipyard in Cumbria. HMS *Sheffield* and ARA *Hercules*, as they were known when commissioned were then on opposite sides in the 1982 Falklands Conflict (not a war). *Sheffield* was sunk, *Hercules* is still on active service.

The first Falklands Crisis had been in 1770 when a Spanish force, also setting off from Argentina, invaded the islands. The Falklands Conflict of 1982 started when an Argentina force invaded the islands on 4/2*.

---

* The second of April is 4/2 when using the date notation known as 'middle endian'—I promise I'm not making this up—which goes mm/dd/yyyy rather than the logical dd/mm/yyyy. The middle endian system is fashionable in the USA and almost nowhere else in the world.

EVERYTHING YOU WISELY REFRAINED FROM ASKING ABOUT THE WHYTE NOTATION

4-2-0

JERVIS
SPOTTING POTENTIAL: NONE

0-6-0T

LBSCR E2 'THOMAS'
SPOTTING POTENTIAL: NONE

BB

CLASS 42 'WARSHIP'
SPOTTING POTENTIAL: 2 SURVIVE

Blood On The Wrong Side of The Tracks

A deed performed by an an American, Frederick Methvan Whyte, has been of inestimable timesaving value to all those interested in chatting about the number of wheels on a train. Since around 1900, railway engineers no longer needed to turn to one another to exclaim 'Hey! Did you just see that! No little wheels! Six big wheels! No little wheels!' Instead, without fuss or drama they have been employing the Whyte Notation to describe Thomas the Tank Engine as being an example of a 0-6-0T configuration—the 'T' denoting Tank and not Thomas. Of course.

EXTREME DANGER. The Whyte Notation works logically when reading the wheels from left to right as you stand facing the left-hand side of the locomotive i.e. with the cow-catcher pointing off to your left. On its right-hand side a 4-2-0 would appear to have become a 0-2-4! Under no circumstances should you go over the rails to identify a train travelling in the other direction—you would place yourself in extreme danger of being seen coming from the wrong side of the tracks which would end your hopes of winning invites to snack at dinner parties with sophisticated and intelligent people. Avoiding potentially fatal social *faux pas* takes real determination. There is no substitute, I've found, for doing up the top toggle of your duffle coat, pouring hot Vimto from the flask, and standing at the end of the platform to wait for the right locomotive the right way round.

Rainbows

The light that makes a rainbow has been refracted-reflected-refracted (bent-bounced-bent) through between 41 and 42 degrees. Did you know:

- There are also moonbows, which have seven colours but appear white
- Looking down from a plane you can see circular rainbows
- You only see one colour from each rain droplet
- In 1987 and aged 42, Richie Blackmore had disbanded Rainbow and was back playing with Deep Purple

From the 42

Much of the world can be viewed through the window of the 42 bus. Catch number 42 to see the following:

See	City	The 42 bus route
The Golden Gate Bridge (on the left)	San Francisco	Richmond to San Rafael
The Eiffel Tower (on the left)	Paris	Gare du Nord to Georges Pompidou European Hospital
Tower Bridge (route crosses the bridge), and Tower 42 (on left, looking up)	London	Denmark Hill to Liverpool Street Station
The CN Tower (on the right)	Toronto	Finch Station to Kennedy Road
Pearl Harbour and the Arizona Memorial (on the left)	Honolulu	Waikiki to Ewa Beach
The monument to the first westbound transatlantic flight by Charles Kingsford-Smith in 1930 (on the left)	Dublin	Downtown Dublin to Portmarnock
42nd Street (part of the 42 route)	New York	Circle Line to East Side

But Why 42?

In the beginning was Ken Welsh

The great hitch-hike began, suitably enough, on the Great Ocean Road at Warrnambool, near Melbourne. In 1966 Ken Welsh and his wife, Ann, had been using travel guidebooks to plan a trip hitchhiking around America and Europe. Five years after sailing from Australia, Ken Welsh (who had been working as a writer for television in Melbourne) had written a guidebook for other hitch-hikers. It was called *Hitch-hiker's Guide to Europe.*

Hitch-hiker's Guide to Europe (without a definite article) is a remarkable book. Obviously not for being a European travel guide. Mariana Starke* had done that a little earlier in 1820, and she was quickly followed by the better known Karl Baedeker**. Nor for inflaming desires to go on self-guided road trips; André

---

* Popularly known as 'Mrs Starke's', the title was *Information and directions for the use of travellers on the continent.* Mrs Starke had introduced a novel idea. Using one to four exclamation marks she summarised her opinion of each attraction. (The news that 186 years later her guide is available to a traveller as a 1.4 Mb ebook downloadable onto a wireless Kindle would, I believe, have moved Mrs Starke into performing a Spinal Tap and nudging her scale to a fifth exclamation mark.)

** The saddest and most ultimately misguided use ever made of a travel guide happened in WWII when Germany, in retaliation for British bombing of historic and popular Lübeck and Rostock, bombed the English provincial towns of Bath, Canterbury, Exeter, Norwich and York—because each had been awarded *drei Stern* in the *Baedeker Tourist Guide to Britain.*

Michelin attended to that when calendars started showing the start of a twentieth century; and Ken and Ann Welsh themselves had 'pored over' Arthur Frommer's *Europe on Five Dollars a Day* before leaving Australia.

No, *Hitch-hiker's Guide to Europe* is remarkable for two other reasons. It was the first guidebook to show the world in a new light. Like the Frommer's guide it was based on practical research giving details of the price of accommodation and meals in US cents and dollars. Very unlike Frommer's the reader was emphatically not a respectful ambassador for her or his country and certainly wasn't, heaven forfend, a *tourist*. Ken Welsh frequently recommended going there now or seeing that soon before each had vanished as the numbers of tourists grew. It was published two years before the first *Lonely Planet Guide* to which it may be compared in voice and style.

'This was at the time of Vietnam and anti-authoritarianism,' Ken Welsh told me when I called to ask when he'd first had the idea for a new kind of travel guide. 'And people had little money.' Anti-authoritarianism meant the travel was about exploring an alternative life as much as reaching any one destination, and the voice speaking from the book was that of a fellow hitcher, ahead of you on the road, with practical advice plus some thoughts for when lifts were slow about the philosophy of travel, happiness and life. By hitching the travelling was being seen to be done in the most alternative and unpredictable way possible. It was the heterodoxy to today's gapper trekking an itinerary worked out with one of our experienced friendly representatives in the specialist call-centre with mum's credit card and amazing I've still got five bars on my mobby now here's one of me, Cordelia and Tatiana leaning over the edge of Tierra del Fuego... Then, even the journey home was an option. Australians Ken and Ann Welsh were to make Spain their home. They live there still.

Summer of 1971: In the news: The first lunar rover was driven on the moon. A US table-tennis team had gotten an invitation to play in China on the say of leader Mao Zedong, to be followed by Henry Kissinger, to be followed by President Nixon—a man focussed on the effect of his failure to end the war in Vietnam on his potential for re-election in 18 months. The construction guys had just done finishing off a multi-use development in Foggy Bottom, Washington D.C. called Watergate. Ozzie

Osbourne and Black Sabbath released a 42-minute album, *Paranoid*, the first song was an anti-Vietnam message called *War Pigs*. Hundreds were suddenly imprisoned without trial in Northern Ireland. A court listening to the Oz obscenity trial had heard the judge say that losing defendant Felix Dennis—publisher, poet and philanthropist—had 'limited ability'. Woodstock and the Isle of Wight 1969 music festivals were the collective fading memory of hippy idealism. Douglas Adams was looking forward to seeing the release of the first Monty Python film. Abbie Hoffman, who lead and symbolized anti-Vietnam protest nailed the paradox facing an alternative society, and simultaneously topped the list of unbeatable book titles, with three words: *Steal This Book*. And Pan published a new book called *Hitch-hiker's Guide to Europe*, which in a deft marketing stroke became the book most often stolen from libraries.

The second reason the first hitch-hiker's guide is remarkable is that it was to be the direct inspiration for *The Hitch-hiker's Guide to The Galaxy*. Douglas Adams told often the story of how he had borrowed a copy of Ken Welsh's book as an *aide-de-camping* while travelling in Europe in the summer between leaving school and tel 01 359 1056

110a Highbury New Park
London N5
19th April

Dear Ken,

Thank you very much for your letter, I was delighted to hear from you. I'd always meant to get in touch with you myself, just to say thanks. Your book was really very useful to me when I used to do a lot of hitching. Europe On Five Dollars a Day was never any use to me because I didn't have that much money and it weighed too much. One day I got frantically depressed in Innsbruck, and lay down in a field as drunk as I could afford to be, which wasn't very. I wanted to leave so I looked through your book, but couldn't find anywhere else I wanted to be (it was the world's fault, and the day's fault, not your books). When the stars came out I thought that someone ought to write a Hitch Hiker's Guide to The Galaxy because it looked a lot more attractive out there than it did around me. That title came back to me years later in a slightly less jaundiced mood, and it turned out to be the best idea (or at least the most profitable) I'd ever had. So one way or another I have a great deal to be grateful to your book for, and I am very happy to be able to give it a plug whenever I get the opportunity.

Thank you for your standing invitation, I shall certainly take you up on it if I find myself in your part of the world. By the same token, if you're in London, give me a call and we'll get together.

Hope to see you here or there,
Best wishes,

Douglas Adams.

going to Cambridge. Later on he said that the telling had been so frequent that he had begun to doubt the veracity himself. A thank you letter written to Ken Welsh in 1981 expressing his gratitude for the book confirms perfectly the details and adds a darker side describing his mood on the night as 'frantically depressed' and 'jaundiced' having had a bad day, and liking neither his surroundings in Innsbruck nor the idea of heading off anywhere else. Douglas Adams' 'most profitable' idea seems to have come out of an attack of the grumps. We are getting slightly ahead of ourselves here so we will pick up on more details of the relationship between the two hitch-hikers guides later but first it is important to understand exactly what it was about *Hitch-hiker's Guide to Europe* that made it worth Douglas Adams tucking it into his rucksack.

Life on the Road in 1971

Chapter One of *Hitch-hiker's Guide to Europe* is called *On the Road.* The same name as Jack Kerouac's milestone of roadlit. The point being that the road itself was a destination. It was where you could experience 'pure chance' and see 'infinite miles of tarmac' which were the 'magic ribbon...to a thousand other worlds'. Hitching was 'an attitude'. The idealism of hitching was grounded by the need for bread or cash, and especially so in countries where work permits were tricky, which was most, and a major theme is the supply of essentials such as cigarettes, alcohol, dope, and maybe a little food if there should be anything over that day.

The sub-title was 'Seeing Europe by skin of your teeth' and you had reached enamel when your living expenses including smokes were a dollar a day. This is about ten dollars (£6.50) today which will cover you for twenty Rothmans in the UK but not a lot else. Richer hitchers could live in style, even kipping in cheap hotels and generally living the life of a total Sybarite, for $5 a day. Spain was ideal, the book noted cigarettes at six cents a pack, wine at four cents a glass and *tapas* for six cents apiece. And the tone was nothing if not liberal. Should hitchers feel the Hemingway thing (Ernest, not Wayne) the wise way to enjoy cattle undergoing cruel and unusual deaths was to invest two or even three dollars on having a seat in the shade and so see suffering in comfort.

Hitching in Europe 1971

A high spot for the over 40s	Seeing the Little Mermaid, Copenhagen
Antwerp, Belgium	Not madly exciting
Athens	Keep away from the cops
Danish pornography	Worth half an hour of anyone's time
Earning money in Paris	Chalk a huge abstract on the pavement
Essen, West Germany	Hell for hitch-hikers
Fez, Morocco	Don't miss Fez
Free beer, food, cigs	Amstel Brewery, Amsterdam
Geneva, Switzerland	No place for $2-a-day hitch-hikers
Greek	A language you don't conquer overnight. Or at all
Ouzo	A drink just right for setting you on your ear
Price to sell your blood for	At least $3/half-litre (Watch they don't take more)
Scandinavian women	Unbelievable. In the spectrum of legend
Free sleeps in central Paris	Montparnasse cemetery. Convenient for everything
Spanish wine	A pleasant way to kill yourself
Spetses, Greece	Not as messed up as Hydra
Stedelijk, Amsterdam	A mind-bender
Taverna to Perivoli, Athens	Great if you're with a bird
Torremolinos, Spain	Nothing to distinguish it from Miami
Vatican City, Rome	Imports food, and exports a nebulous hope

Based on: *Hitch-hiker's Guide to Europe*, Ken Welsh, 1971

Interested in sex? Torremolinos was one place amongst several you should head, it being 'inundated with people looking for someone to hook up with for a couple of weeks'. If you wouldn't or couldn't commit to that kind of long-term relationship Amsterdam at night was described as one of the great free sights in Europe and where fifteen minutes of 'mostly indifference' could be had for four dollars. For another form of recreation the cheapest marijuana was in Ketama in the Rif Mountains where the dope was that Moroccan grass should be haggled down to $50 a kilo. This knowledge was accompanied with sage advice to bulk-buying herbalists that near Hercules' other pillar hitchers were—and how unfair could life get—being targetted by Spanish border officials for 'random' searches.

Other than advising women not to hitch alone dangers were almost not worthy of much consideration. The greatest risk was of being in a car smash caused by a generous but dangerously nifty lift-donor. Hitch-hikers were not carrying a mountain of mp3 players, phones, cameras, notebook computers, money, plastic or towels (a towel was not included in the guide's what-to-take list), and so were of quite limited interest to any larcenously-minded locals. But the police in Greece were certainly to be feared, and later editions reported also on just how simple it was to find six years free accommodation in a Turkish prison. As *na Trioblóidi* (the Troubles) escalated in Northern Ireland a warning was added to the guide counselling hitchers to think twice before going there as travelling could be 'dangerous'.

The Best Lunch in the Universe

The best lunch in the universe happened on Friday. Twenty-four year old Douglas Adams' attempts at comic writing had been quite comprehensively failing for the worst part of three years and increasingly an unacceptable idea had to be faced—maybe he wasn't going to make it as a writer; and an unpleasant number—his overdraft—had forced a retreat home to darkest Dorset which, as everyone he really needed to impress knew, was just over a million parsecs away from London. Fortunately someone was interested. His name was Simon Brett, a radio producer who had used and liked a Douglas Adams' sketch in a zanywackyandpythonesqueinstyle radio show called *The Burkiss Way*. The Brett Insight, which we need to be thankful for, was that the tyro's potential lay in writing longer rather than shorter. And so Simon Brett invited Douglas Adams to come up to London on Friday February 4th 1977 for lunch in a Japanese restaurant bringing three radio show ideas.

One of the ideas sitting at the table, and quite frankly struggling a little with the chop-sticks, was a science fiction comedy series. The original idea had been six stand-alone programs each of which ended the world in an amusing way, for example, being demolished to make space for a new bypass. This idea, Simon Brett liked. Which was quite a surprise to Douglas Adams—for almost three years he had been trying to engage with a brain in BBC TV, and any brain in BBC TV would have been good, regarding his ideas for a science fiction comedy.

Working on how a first episode might work on radio included choosing a means of feeding the plot, one line of thinking being to have an alien already on earth, and a logical reason for extra-terrestrials to drop by would be when publishers of galactic hitch-hiker's guides sent their researchers out periodically. From here it was one more leap to begin thinking that this might work rather well as a developing story over six episodes rather than six separate stories.

And so, in Dorset Douglas Adams produced four sheets* of paper which were to be the first of many millions bearing the

---

* Three are reproduced in *Don't Panic*, Neil Gaiman's biography of Douglas Adams. Above Douglas Adams' name is a schoolbook margin drawing of the constellation of Ursa Major. The neatly typed effect created by neatly typing had been sacrificed during the taxi ride to the big meeting at the BBC with the star's name, one Aleric B, being crossed out, several times, and replaced with the hand-written *Arthur Dent*. One has to wonder where Aleric B is now? Might there have been a spot of bother? The actors' union Equity has no record of him.

words: *The Hitch-hiker's Guide to The Galaxy*. The document was presented at a meeting with a commissioning group at BBC Radio, a group that, heigh-ho, included Simon Brett, and it came to pass that on March 1st 1977 Douglas Adams received news that his pilot show would be commissioned, and with which tidings of great joy a manual typewriter in darkest Dorset aided by Douglas Adams aided by tea and sandwiches from his mum wrote the first episode of *The Hitch-hiker's Guide to The Galaxy*. It can be examined in the BBC's *Original Radio Scripts* and is polished writing that zings along with all the character, humour, style, ideas, voice, humour, special effects, music and much else of what was to come. The pilot script was delivered to Simon Brett on the 4th April. Eight weeks had passed since the best lunch in the universe.

Picture This

After completing the pilot script the weeks that followed were to be almost the last when Douglas Adams wasn't under a deadline to write something. Three months were spent waiting for the pilot show to be made after which a further month passed and then on the first day of August 1977 the life-changing commission arrived asking for five more like this, please, adding that recordings would be starting in October. Picture a happy and relaxed Douglas Adams with the thought bubble above his head thinking 'plenty of time'. Now picture, if it is possible, a Tardis-shaped bluebottle buzzing straight down into a bowl of delicious Dorset Cream.

Suddenly, Douglas Adams had acquired a surfeit of success. It happened because during the long wait for news of possible radio work he had approached, most wisely you might think, the BBC's *Doctor Who* team with a view to parlaying the triumph of getting a pilot radio script commissioned into further work writing for the venerable television sci-fi medical drama. Nothing succeeding like success this succeeded in spades. Just ahead of the commission for the five radio scripts a potentially even more important commission had arrived—to write an outline with a view to writing a whole *Doctor Who* television series. There was no thought of delaying either project. The TV outline needed to be completed by the end of August which Douglas Adams achieved by sacrificing a month of his anticipated schedule on *The Hitch-hiker's Guide to The Galaxy*. The amazing news then arrived that he was now a TV writer and he briefly stepped away from his typewriter to place four new deadlines for the *Doctor*

Who episodes onto the mantelpiece alongside the clock and the five deadlines for radio scripts that he could hear quietly a-ticking—Douglas Adams had gone from no deadlines to ten deadlines in a time that would impress a particularly pacy particle accelerator.

Forwarding-fast: Douglas Adams' plan to write *Doctor Who* and *The Hitch-hiker's Guide to The Galaxy* and keep to deadlines now ticking loudly enough to bring the council round was more than improbable. Schedules got re-arranged; two of the radio scripts just made it under the wire; and the final *Doctor Who* scripts were a month over schedule, being finished at the end of January. By then there was no longer the kind of time left that Douglas Adams knew he needed to write the two remaining radio scripts for the already revised recording schedule. His solution was to call in a close friend, the producer John Lloyd (who would later make *Spitting Image*, *Blackadder*, *QI*, and Barclaycard ads). The two had shared accommodation since Cambridge days and had also recently written two episodes of a children's TV series. Through February the partnership of Douglas Adams and John Lloyd created episodes five and six of *The Hitch-hiker's Guide to The Galaxy* and recording of the final episode went ahead on the last day of February 1978.

Science Fiction Comedy

While growing up, the young Douglas Adams had experienced vintage years of science fiction. During the sixties and early seventies British television had made *Doctor Who* a sci-fi medical series revolving around the transfer of a Casanova meme gene expressed in middle-aged Englishmen able to travel through time and space hoovering up attractive but often strangely breathless women at will for temporary employ as improbably feckless 'companions'. In the late sixties a major Kubrick film *2001: A Space Odyssey* shrank the achievements of the new brave world of manned space travel into the context of an alien universe full of infinite mystery, including the problem of how best to deal with a lip-reading homebrew psycho known as Hal. In books a teenage read-of-passage was Tolkien's mindworld *The Lord of the Rings,* where human moralities were explored by an everyman with hairy toes and a hectic life jeopardised at every turn in a longish hunt for mislaid jewellery. And back to television, *Star Trek* was the way to really go when you needed to intelligently join an argument about whether infinitives could ever be too boldly split.

Comic writing as precious as even a Douglas Adams'

sketch would commonly have been wiped or lost in an archive. The lightning-fast success of *The Hitch-hiker's Guide to The Galaxy* has meant that five Douglas Adams' sketches were kept and are now available within a 3-CD compilation called *Douglas Adams at the BBC*. These include a brief excerpt of Douglas Adams on *Desert Island Discs* and some of his *Doctor Who* work. The sketches are transfused with comedy blood straight from the absurdist artery. This vessel had first been nicked on radio by *The Goon Show* before being arteriotomised one-handed by Spike Milligan in *Q5*, and then radically dissected by The Pythons—who reached an absurdist extreme point of some kind with the cheerful blood-bath they called *Sam Peckinpah's 'Salad Days'*.

The sketch by Douglas Adams called *Eric von Contrick* is the most remarkable. It is very close to being the progenitor of *The Hitch-hiker's Guide to The Galaxy*. Commissioned in 1976 for *The Burkiss Way* by Simon Brett it may also have been the first professional writing commission for Douglas Adams whose embryonic professional credentials must have been stretched when it was apparently delivered late by... forty two days. Light-bulbs would prove easier to change than spots on this leopard.

An irony of ironies in Douglas Adams' legendary specialist career in deadlines (the missing of) is that the acme of the arc of his talents was timing his comedy. *Star Wars*—the international prototype kilogram of heavyweight blockbuster science fiction—was released in the UK at the end of 1977 with enormous publicity just as *The Hitch-hiker's Guide to The Galaxy* was being recorded and produced. A few weeks later at the UK première of Steven Spielberg's *Close Encounters of the Third Kind* the lady at the titular head of the queue in the London Odeon for having her ticket torn—and with the royal command of 'Phil, shotgun front' getting first dibs on seats proximate to the screen—was also the head of state, Her Majesty Queen Elizabeth II. This was only five days after the monarch and consort had clustered around the Buckingham Palace radio—most likely—to listen to the first episode of *The Hitch-hiker's Guide to The Galaxy*. The new rock and roll was science fiction and, thanks to his incredibly good timing, Douglas Adams was in the band.

The *Eric von Contrick* sketch parodies an interview with best-selling-books-about-aliens author, Eric von Daniken. It starts by establishing von Contrick's cynicism before being 'interrupted' by the landing of an alien craft right beside the BBC which is reported live in a parody of the approach of the aliens in Orson Welles' *War of the Worlds*. The alien leader, Ulom B (heard as a sound effect of repeated 'B's) of the Race of your Forefathers from the Galaxy of Smegma demands that Eric von Contrick returns a fluffy kitten from which the human race had descended. Cut into the reportage on Earth's first visitors is the radio interviewer's personal agenda as he bitches about the perceived airs and graces acquired when ex-radio colleagues ascend to the sunlit uplands of television. This first Douglas Adams' comedy science fiction script could have time-warped back from somewhere in any of the first episodes of *The Hitch-hiker's Guide to The Galaxy*.

And introducing...42

Numbers are distinctively a part of Douglas Adams' comedy. Four of the five preserved BBC sketches make use of numbers for humorous effect. One of these is a sketch called *The Kamikaze Pilot* which was also commissioned at the lunch with Simon Brett which lead to *The Hitch-hiker's Guide to The Galaxy*. The sketch, co-written with Chris Keightley originally for a 1976 Cambridge revue, features the debriefing of serially unsuccessful Kamikaze pilot, Simpkins (sounding not completely unlike Peter Sellers), on the 'abominable' details of each of his nineteen failed suicide missions.

The first time that Douglas Adams and forty two got it together seems to be in an earlier sketch with the title of *Hole in The Wall Club*. This had been written in 1974 for a Cambridge revue by Douglas Adams with two other Cambridge students in a team calling themselves Adams-Smith-Adams. The show and the sketch were well-received, making it onto the London stage and TV. These performances were by a portion of the Cambridge Footlights cast, a portion that did not include Douglas Adams, who for a while had been beyond bitter about not having been chosen as a performer. His great and burning ambition at the time had been to become a writer-performer in the exact mould of John Cleese and this was a major blow. Those on stage included Clive Anderson and Griff Rhys Jones, a Welsh schoolmate of Douglas Adams—having together performed in the Scottish Play called *Macbeth*—and it was to be Griff Rhys Jones who delivered a line of more than usual significance (in the sketch, not the Scottish Play called *Macbeth*). In 1974 he announced, in a Douglas Adams co-written line that he was about to read: '…the minutes of the 42nd meeting of the Crawley and District Paranoid Society'.

Douglas Adams used forty two for a second time in a sketch called *23 Gunga Din Crescent* which is six pints of hyper-oxygenated type-A rhesus-positive EPO-elevated Monty Python. A film crew set up at the eponymous address of the title in unremarkable Sawbridgeworth believing 'a sketch may happen today'. Forced to report on minutiae they are eventually told by the occupier, Mrs Thomas, that their mark, a Mrs Bus-Stop Bass-Peekee-Noin-Kyne Cuttlefish is round at 42 Logical Positivism Avenue. Enthusiasts planning a trip for the weekend need to know that unremarkable Sawbridgeworth has neither a Gunga Din Crescent nor a Logical Positivism Avenue. The sketch aired on *The Burkiss Way* two days prior to the lunch with Simon Brett.

Douglas Adams planned numbers carefully. The numbers he chose for the first six radio episodes are remarkably diverse and are shown in Appendix Z. Some of the world's funniest integers are meeting for the first time. 53 from the book title *53 More Things to Do In Zero Gravity*; $2^{267,209}$ in the odds of $2^{267,209}$ to one against being picked up in space and of course the phone number of the Islington flat; and the 573 of the 573 committee meetings that had yet failed to invent fire. But, Douglas Adams didn't use four as either a first or last interesting digit (zero not being interesting) in any of his double-digit or greater numbers deployed prior to forty-two. The probability of this being chance is 3851 to 1. Flukey, maybe—but it looks most improbable given the Adams' propensity for carefully selecting numbers and taste for forty two. The finger of suspicion must point to the eventual use of the forty two joke being planned around the time that either the pilot episode or possibly the second episode were being written and that the pitch was kept clear of any similar sounding number to heighten the drama for the ultimate moment when Deep Thought said: 'Forty two.' Multiple appearances of forty two within the carefully chosen words of Douglas Adams—plum character roles in two sketches prior to playing the lead in *The Hitch-hiker's Guide to The Galaxy*—looks, I'm switching Oscar Wilde about here, a lot like carefulness.

So, Why? 42…

By speaking here and there, being interviewed at regular intervals and appearing on TV and radio, Douglas Adams was an upstanding example of everything you could ever wish to see in your writing superstars. Retiring, reclusive, difficult, he was not. But…in twenty three years spent offering comment and insight on much else of import he spoke directly on the origins of forty two only in a particular way. The gist always being that Douglas Adams declined the opportunity to provide the full story behind why forty two was chosen ahead of similarly 'deadpan' unfunny numbers. And quite rightly so, magicians fond of telling it like it is about the prestidigitation involved in covertly inserting the ace of spades into the rabbit are thin on the ground nowadays. A collection of Douglas Adams' explanations and those of two significant others are wodged inside a carrier bag (Caecum A) lodged under the stairs if you should care to go through the evidence. The possibilities can be shaken into eight groups: it was an unfunny sounding number; it was a funny sounding number; it was designed to mean something; it was a random number; he copied it; it meant something to Douglas Adams; it was something else I haven't thought of; and various combinations of those—except being random with any of the others.

Popular Theory

Popular theories about the meaning of why the Ultimate Answer was forty two have multiplied through time, the list includes; being the age of Elvis Presley when he died, the length of the traditional list of rulers of Tibet, the answer you get when multiplying six by nine in base thirteen, as you do, the number with which the earth is created in Kabbalistic tradition, reversing the digits of Douglas Adams age when he was commissioned to write the first episode, the net angle through which light is reflected and refracted in a rainbow, the code on Douglas Adams' English library books, copying Lewis Carroll who had liked using the number in his writing, the number of principles of ancient Egyptian Ma'at law, the duration in months of the time the beast may have controlled the earth in some versions of the bible, the number you get by adding up the cipher values of the letters D Adams, for tweeting purposes the number of characters in 'answer to life the universe and everything', the number of episodes Douglas Adams had written when the joke was deployed and the number there were still to write, and very sweet—the re-arranged syllables of tea for two. There are more if you need them.

Here Are More

France

- A New Zealand Vodka (42 Below)
- Mr Simpson buys 42 tubs instead of the 50 on special deal
- 42 orcs were slain by either Gimli (book) or Legolas (film)
- Number of the département of the Loire
- 42nd day of the year is February 11
- Number of first robot to visit Will Smith in *I, Robot*
- A pearl wedding in France
- 10/10/10 is World 42 Day as 101010_2 is 42 in binary
- Minimum age of a consul in Rome

German

- 4+2 = sex
- DB (Deutsche Bahn) is a cover for forty two
- A Cheops pyramid grave number
- Age of Pierce Brosnan in *Goldeneye*
- Bill Clinton is the officially listed 42nd President
- God in German is 42 in cipher (g=7 & so on)
- Fox Mulder lives in Apartment 42
- ...and the Pope's size in red shoes

Australia

- Asteroid DA42 was given the official name Douglas Adams
- The GNU C library memfrob() performs an XOR with 42 (this one wins the special prize)
- 42 is a Coldplay track
- Strigaskór nr. 42 is an Icelandic band
- Episode 42 of *Doctor Who* is 42 minutes
- 42 is Buzz Lightyear's spaceship
- An LP of then fictional band Level 42 is in *A Clockwork Orange*
- The favourite number of House MD
- Maximum number of studs in Lego games is 42×10^8
- 42nd issue of *Stuff* magazine deliberately omitted from sequence
- Appears on a shoe in *Amelie*
- Monty Python's *How Not To Be Seen* sketch (1970) features government information film No. 42

A Big Clue

Once, even Douglas Adams was excited by the possibility that forty two could really mean something big in terms of Life, the Universe and Everything. The knowledge caused him to experience, apparently, the sort of natural high that finds one playfully grasping the lapels of pals to better inform them you'd told them so and you were right all along and they were all fools to doubt you, etc. The time was in 1996 when Cambridge University astronomers announced with a degree of levity atypical of astronomers from Cambridge University that they might have found the Ultimate Answer because their measurements seemed to show that the Hubble Constant was 42. (Not to be confused with the former international cricket umpire David 'Connie' Constant who is 69.)

As you will know, this means that a galaxy one megaparsec distant is shuffling itself further away at forty two kilometres per second which wasn't necessarily something everyone had realised they needed up their sleeves, but for astronomers is their response when your question is 'So, just how fast is the universe falling apart?' Regrettably, if forty two was intended to be the ultimate answer of both cosmic and comic import then no-one texted the universe with a cautious 'mind how you go now', as the Hubble Constant is today thought by a consensus of hot astronomers to be up at around 70 and later this year, after his birthday, risks being mistaken for David Constant.

The significance of the above of course—tenders of grassy-knoll conspiracy theories, hobbit-fanciers and the lightly trepanned might care to sit together and chow down on the dilithium crystals here—isn't that news from Cambridge about the Hubble Constant possibly being forty two and therefore really the Ultimate Answer deeply chuffed Douglas Adams (which is fun to know) but that he didn't argue with, contradict, or automatically gainsay the proposition with a pile of his own evidence stacked along the lines of '...well I just happen to know different, being the oracle and that'.

Sparking Ideas

There was a pause of almost six years between the Innsbruck field Big Bang when Douglas Adams first thought that someone should write *The Hitch-hiker's Guide to The Galaxy* and finding that the someone was himself and that now in front of the someone were four pages of blank paper anxious to carry great ideas describing a comedy radio series to the BBC.

One of the first places that Douglas Adams sought his inspiration was the borrowed copy of Ken Welsh's *Hitch-hiker's Guide to Europe* that had accompanied him across Europe to Istanbul and back (it wasn't entirely the greatest of trips—in Istanbul he was ill and returned by train rather than hitching). The Guide to Hitch-hiker's Guides shows that the original radio series of *The Hitch-hiker's Guide to The Galaxy* and Ken Welsh's *Hitch-hiker's Guide to Europe* share a number of ideas and also shows from where some of the 'sparks from the grindstone', as Douglas Adams once described his ideas, had originated.

Guide to Hitch-hiker's Guides

Europe (1971)	Galaxy (1978)
The Original	The me-too radio shows, records, cassettes, CDs, trilogy, stage shows, radio scripts, comics, audiobooks, TV series, film, DVDs, kindle editions, plus towels
The first sentence explains that the book is designed to show you how to get around Europe for about twenty-five dollars a week—cheaper if you're tough enough	[Original synopsis and Episode One] Ford explains that the purpose of the guide is to help impoverished hitch-hikers see the marvels of the Galaxy for less than thirty Altairian dollars a day
Forty-seven countries are covered, many with a deal of precise information. These are balanced by Albania's entry that simply says 'Forget it.'	[Original synopsis and Episode One] The original entry for Earth is 'Harmless'. Ford gets this enlarged. To 'Mostly harmless' [Episode One] And, if you want a lift from a Vogon: 'Forget It.'
THE ONLY BOOK TO TELL YOU EVERYTHING YOU NEED TO KNOW And so quite a bargain. This is on the back cover near the price of (7/-) 35p. (Britain had converted to decimal currency in February.)	[Episode One] Ford Prefect declares that *The Hitch-hiker's Guide to the Galaxy* will tell you everything you want to know. (On the radio the narrator was telling you.)

Europe (1971)	**Galaxy (1978)**
The 'unfashionable' reason for Australians and Americans to visit England is to see the Mother Country	[Episode Two] Our apparently un-regarded sun is in the uncharted backwaters of the unfashionable end of the Western spiral arm of the Galaxy
For all their worldly goods and social benefits the bulk of the people are bored—the common complaint of Scandinavian students	[Episode Two] Most of the people living on Earth were unhappy for most of the time
What-to-see-in-Oslo recommends the Norwegian Design Centre which offers '...all that's good in Norwegian design'	[Episodes Three & Four] Slartibartfast, who—as we all know—designs coastlines, got an award for Norway
In Lyon? Visit the Museum of Fine Arts to view Gauguin's *Who are we? Whence do we come? Whither are we going?* (Hitching there today to see Polynesians musing the Meaning of Life will elicit a fourth question; 'Where is it?', as the masterpiece hangs in the Boston Museum of Fine Arts)	[Episode Four] The narrator orates on the meaning of life: 'Why are people born?', 'Why do they die?', and 'Why do they want to spend so much of the intervening time wearing digital watches?'

Of particular interest to alert Albanian readers will be the new knowledge that their whole country's meriting of just a two word entry in *Hitch-hiker's Guide to Europe* ('ALBANIA—Forget it.') was to doubly-inspire Douglas Adams. The economical sentence is the same as the advice in *The Hitch-hiker's Guide to The Galaxy* on what to do if you want to get a lift from a Vogon ('Forget it.') and terse brevity on a grand scale was of course the original joke about Ford Prefect managing to double the word count of the entry for planet Earth in *The Hitch-hiker's Guide to The Galaxy*—Earth leaping from 'Harmless' to 'Mostly harmless' being where the four-page synopsis ended.

This is not to say that the Vogons are Albanian. Ask the Vogon psyche to stand shoulder to shoulder with the other nationals described in *Hitch-hiker's Guide to Europe* and their mental physiognomy—a love of bureaucracy and loathing of hitch-hikers—matches descriptions of most of the communist states but fits perfectly with the description of the lengthy procedure to be followed to even stand a chance of entering the USSR (this required the date of entry and of exit, and the purpose of visit being stated for every town on the planned journey, with a rider that hitch-hiking is not encouraged). The Vogons were Russian.

The Special Page

Ken Welsh's opinion about one country seems…different. The first page of the country-by-country section of *Hitchhiker's Guide to Europe* introduces the British Isles and Ireland with insights rarely or never seen in any other travel guide for young Americans and Australians (sorry, no Kiwis) thinking of their first trip to England: 'a lot of her people…can't afford a train fare'; 'minds ...turned inwards…to fight the ogre of survival against over-population'; 'gasping cities', 'solid wall of bus, lorry, car and train fumes…as healthy as the next cubic mile of poison'; 'nearly pure carbon monoxide'; 'dirty, cancerous, black-faced London'. It must have bemused Douglas Adams to read of this London. Ken Welsh explained to me he had been shocked at the difference with his experience living in a beautiful, seaside, Australian small town.

He ascribes young Americans and Antipodeans thinking of visiting England with a very sound reason and a very unfashionable reason. The sound reason being that it was about the easiest place to be able to work. The very unfashionable reason was that England could be seen to be the object of 'an Oedipus Complex' being the Motherland to the former colonies. He wrote:

'...she still offers the solution to the most puzzling question of all: where did our families come from?

'Plenty of people find the answer a little disappointing.'

Not liking the answer to the most puzzling question of all—might seem familiar to listeners and readers of *The Hitch-hiker's Guide to The Galaxy*. If this is the point of singularity before the Big Bang of expansion into Douglas Adams' Ultimate Question and Answer to Life, the Universe and Everything then I am so pleased to be able to tell you that it is on page forty two of *Hitch-hiker's Guide to Europe*.

Thrice 42

To have used forty two three times over in two sketches and Hitch-hikers within three years seems to confirm the explanations Douglas Adams gave for his having chosen forty two (Caecum A). He maintained that it had not been essential for the number to be forty two, being selected simply as an unfunny number—intended for maximum humorous effect in Deep Thought's deadpan, bathetic, *non sequitur* punchline.

The popular yearning for forty two to have some deeper significance and not be simply taken at face value as an unfunny number can perhaps be attributed to human nature. There is a part of many of us that favours the mystery of a conspiracy theory over an inconveniently mundane truth. The prevalence of the desire to suspect that 'there must be more' would appear to posit a belief that there had once been and still could be, evolutionary advantage for humans to be naturally disbelieving. For example, a majority of 72% of adults in the UK believe that the United States may have, or definitely has, a department that creates false conspiracy theories to discredit genuine conspiracy theories (Appendix X). Almost two in three (64%) believe that the US administration may be or is hiding facts about the 1947 Roswell alien and almost the same proportion (62%) have a similar level of assuredness that the CIA was responsible for killing President Kennedy. Proving negatives—usually the bottom-line for refuting conspiracy theories—is commonly impossible. Once it's rolling, a conspiracy theory or a there-must-be-more belief defies the second law of thermodynamics being happily self-sustaining without further informational nourishment. Denial is futile.

The proportion of 75% of readers of Douglas Adams who believe that forty two was chosen because it had a meaning (Appendix Y) is similar to the proportion of the population that tends to favour the existence of conspiracy theories. One in four readers of Douglas Adams believe that forty two does not have special meaning and of the reasons prompted the one most likely to be believed, by one in five, was that forty two had been the page number in *Hitch-hiker's Guide to Europe* where there was a most puzzling question with a disappointing answer.

For Douglas Adams there was a deeper and inherently uncomfortable side to an ordinarily innocuous question about families in the plural. An area of his life he spoke of sparingly was the time at the age of five (with a little sister of two) when their parents' relationship had deteriorated beyond being able to live under one roof—even though there were two young children and divorce was less common than it is nowadays. Although both were to remarry and both had more children, feelings in the future between his mother and father were to remain quite unpleasant. As a result, for nearly all of his life Douglas Adams lived with two families instead of a family. He loved and got on very well with his new siblings but clearly nothing was ever the same. The saddest word I heard Douglas Adams use in the course of my research was his description of having felt like 'a shuttlecock' when being ferried, with his sister, between the two families, often by their maternal grandmother.

Two questions remain unanswered: how, and when, Douglas Adams first came to know that forty two was particularly effective as an unfunny number.

Douglas Adams: Seer

Consider the Altair. A computer Jim, but not as we know it. Twenty-four dinky little red lights substitute for a display screen. Sixteen teeny-tiny metal flick switches stand in for a keyboard. The memory could remember the first four lines of this paragraph before reaching a point referred to between computers as 'sorry, my brain's full'. There was a manual. The manual assumed you knew about soldering and stuff because you were ankle-deep in chips and cards and wires and little red lights and teeny-tiny switches. You were going to assemble the first personal computer from a kit that had just arrived by mail order because you posted a cheque for

$439 to Albuquerque, of all places, following the excitement of seeing a picture of a grey box with little red lights and teeny-tiny switches, saying 'Altair 8800', that was splashed over the cover of your January 1975 copy of *Popular Electronics*. It was actually a mock-up—never trust anything you read, and only half of what you see. Augurs of a revolution about to change much of the world that are more immediately recognisable can be imagined.

A Jimi Hendrix fan in Boston saw the magazine and told a friend of the forthcoming revolution. The two were excited, but instead of a cheque they just mailed a letter. Paul Allen (21), the Jimi Hendrix fan, and Bill Gates (19) deduced that if even the smartest of new friends was only capable of chatting in hexadecimal ('hex' 42 means 66—the system lacks the potential for humour) even the most loving of geek-computer relationships might become strained and would soon create a yearning for something resembling plain English.

Their letter arrived on the desk of Ed Roberts, inventor of the Altair, offering to show him a program that would let his customers use their new Altairs more easily via a computer language called Basic. A dialogue followed. They had a working program? Yes—actually meaning to say not as such, or at all. Nor did they have an Altair on which to test their programming. On the other hand Ed Roberts was, a) speaking from under a rapidly growing New Mexico snowdrift of Altair 8800 orders and, b) would first have to work on beefing up the size of the Altair's brain before Paul Allen and Bill Gates' program could have a chance to work. A mutually convenient date for a demonstration was diarised for March 1975.

Many things are taught at Harvard University but 2nd year student Bill Gates was self-taught in the skills needed to use the big university computer for personal business purposes. By instructing its considerably-sized brain to become, for a few moments, a baby Altair brain they were able to test their program so that, hopefully, the demonstration in Albuquerque would work. The story then goes that when the big day arrived and Paul Allen flew to Albuquerque with a precious roll of punched paper bearing the program he lacked the cash to pay for his hotel room and was subbed by his potential client. The story further goes that the demonstration ran perfectly and that the first test of Altair Basic was some simple arithmetic:

2+2=?

4

Lives then followed different arcs. Paul Allen and Bill Gates formed Microsoft and became two of the richest billionaires* in the world. Ed Roberts the talented engineer whose ideas and Altair design were very quickly copied by many others within a couple of years had sold the company and aged forty returned to being the medical student he had first planned on becoming twenty years earlier. When he qualified he became a country doctor in Georgia. He died there in 2010. Bill Gates had travelled to see him when he had become unwell.

Finding 2+2 equalled 4 in Albuquerque was one of the most important moments in modern history. We had a cheap computer. We had a program. We could produce data. We were on our way somewhere but no-one saw that within their lifetimes the money then to be made from the picks (a useable Altair was $1000) and shovels (Altair Basic was $75) could ever be challenged by the data which just didn't look like gold

---

* Paul Allen has donated a considerable sum to a project in-part searching for extra-terrestrial life and based at the University of California, Berkeley. Choosing to reference Douglas Adams, the first phase of development for the Allen Telescope Array required 42 radio telescopes.

(4 being worth $0). Ed Roberts sold the Altair business in 1977 for two million dollars, Micro-soft was growing fast by selling programs to the Altair's competition, and two boys had turned five years old. Their names were Larry Page and Sergey Brin and the two, as you probably know, were soon to found the phenomenon of data made into gold known as Google.

The Enid

Where could we be without digression? The British children's author, Enid Blyton, operating at the top of her game in 1943 was the first person to have thought of Google and after a profitable morning had pencilled in most of the afternoon for resolving the Riemann hypothesis, buttoning down the more nebulous areas of M-theory, fettling the Lampard-Gerrard paradox, and finding a Higgs' boson or three before making a nice cold tongue and beetroot sandwich when in a moment of loss to science of dimensions unmeasurable her publisher called to say the spread-betting on next year's Man Booker prize was moving towards the winning novel being about the thraldom of four children by a dæmon hound they knew as Timmy and could you possibly run something up if the weird sciency book went to one side for a couple of ticks, Enid?

The End

Improbable as it sounds, until 1982 with regard to all things computers Douglas Adams described himself as having been a 'technophobe'. The improbability is compounded by his having achieved the unlikely feat of including references to both the Altair and Google together in 1977 in the first radio series of *The Hitch-hiker's Guide to The Galaxy*. Google wasn't registered as a word for a further twenty or more years.

The Altair reference is made in the guide's proclamation of containing helpful advice on seeing the universe for less than thirty Altairian dollars a day. This reference was to both the new breed of micro computers and the star from which the computer's name had been taken. The Google link comes with Douglas Adams being first to use the word Googleplex. This is the name of Google's headquarters at Mountain View, San Francisco: dial 94043 into Google Earth and you can look down on Building 42 where the CEO of Google, Eric Schmidt, has chosen to locate his office.

In *The Original Radio Scripts* the word googleplex is italicised, having been edited out to fit the airtime but the mention of the Googleplex Starthinker re-appears, slightly modified, in the book as the Googleplex Star Thinker; one of the most powerful computers in the universe, able to calculate the trajectories of all the sand particles in a five week sand blizzard—but a mere pocket calculator compared to Deep Thought, which can deal with the vectors of all the atoms in the Big Bang.

Douglas Adams' life was not one of continuous creative success. For nearly all the years he spent as one of the best-selling authors in the world there had been plans and meetings and more plans and more meetings to make a Hitch-hiker's film. When he died he was still trying to get the movie made. Four years posthumously the film was released but twenty years of meetings added to twenty years planning seemed to suck away some of the fun.

And through most of the nineties a tremendous endeavour had been working with a part-owned company called The Digital Village to create a speaking computer game called *Starship Titanic*. Understandably players had been sold, and bought into, Douglas-Adams-sized expectations and were underwhelmed when the game was finally ready. A second project foundered and would have sunk when the fin-de-millennium rage for interweb investment went ever-so-slightly off the boil. It was called H2G2 (not especially scrutable as code for *The Hitch-hiker's Guide to The Galaxy*) with many of the forty staff in The Digital Village creating an 'earth edition'. This was to be an online encyclopaedia with the then novel difference of being created, in part, by user submissions. (Douglas Adams was user number 42). The idea was pulled off the rocks by the BBC which continues to fund its existence but it failed to attract a critical mass of contributors, the thing Wikipedia was to achieve and which lead to a naturally growing number of both users and contributors. This then ultimately allows—along with Google—the kind of research needed to assemble a book like this one, which probably wouldn't have been possible, even with almost unlimited time, in the most impressive physical library. This may or may not, of course, be seen as a good thing.

Douglas Adams part predicted and part shaped the future. His funny Babel fish in-ear translator exists in name as an online translation service. But think of it as a step on the road to a translating mobile phone. As a tribute to Deep Thought, Deep Blue was adopted as the name for a computer that beat the world chess champion (inter-game fixes lead to a disputed outcome and a re-match was refused by the computer's agent). And just yesterday in the paper I read that the new Stephen Hawking book explains how you and I are choosing from amongst infinities of histories most of which are highly improbable but all of which extend from the moment of the Big Bang. At that moment I chose to recall the similarity between such an incredible idea and Douglas Adams' explanation of the principle behind his infinite improbability drive.

And if another hitch-hiker's guide in the far future has only a little space to describe the achievements of an ape descendant called Douglas Adams, then that should still be fine. He was the thinker who created the forty two joke. Try googling 'the Answer to Life, the Universe and Everything'. In under zero-point-four-two seconds the Great Google Brain will have allocated your task to a sub-neuron or two, read your question, trailed a finger through an unimaginably long index, then found, written out and posted to you the answer...it is 42. I believe Douglas Adams would have liked that very much indeed.

Appendix X: Conspiracy Theories

Opinions of 1000 UK adults surveyed in June 2010 by The Survey Shop.

Q. Which of the following do you believe are true, or may be true?	**True, or may be true**	**True**
A secret US department creates false conspiracy theories to discredit genuine conspiracy theories.	72%	14%
The US Government is hiding facts about the 1947 Roswell alien	64%	16%
Osama bin Laden is dead	63%	4%
President Kennedy was assassinated by the CIA	62%	7%
The Large Hadron Collider might create a black hole	49%	11%
Time travel will become possible within 100 years	34%	4%
All statistics are false	34%	10%
The Americans did not land on the moon	24%	5%
Hitler faked his death	20%	2%
Elvis Presley is still alive	4%	1%
Michael Jackson is still alive	4%	1%

Appendix Y: Forty two theories

The opinions of 204 adults who had read *The Hitch-hiker's Guide to The Galaxy* and responded that the Answer to Life, the Universe and Everything was forty two. Conducted in June 2010 by The Survey Shop.

Q. The following are valid possible reasons why Douglas Adams chose the number 42 in The Hitch-hiker's Guide to The Galaxy. In your opinion which is most likely to be true and which are either possible or unlikely? (any)	**Most likely to be true**
He had no reason, but it had to be a number he hadn't already used	25%
In the 1971 book which inspired his title, *Hitch-Hiker's Guide to Europe*, page 42 is the first page of the chapter about Britain and Ireland and part of it is devoted to 'the most puzzling question of all'	20%
He was following Lewis Carroll, who liked using forty-two and had a rule 42 in *Alice in Wonderland* and also called *The Hunting of the Snark* an agony in eight fits, meaning parts, just as each radio episodes was also called a fit.	18%
The 42 joke comes towards the end of the fourth of six episodes. He admitted later that after writing the first four at that stage he ran out of ideas for the last two episodes	14%

Douglas Adams was struggling to succeed when at the age of 24 the BBC agreed to the first pilot radio show and he switched the digits of that special age	7%
As an English student he had been used to seeing the library code 420 on his books at university	4%
Elvis Presley died at the age of 42 with enormous media coverage at the same time that Douglas Adams was writing the radio scripts	4%
As a teenager, his father had a 'James Bond' type Aston Martin DB5. D and B are the 4th and 2nd letters of the alphabet	2%

Appendix Z: Numerology of the Hitch-hiker's Guide

To show the numbers at work in *The Hitch-hiker's Guide to the Galaxy* the plug in the bottom of the Marianas trench has been pulled out to allow all the words and single digit numbers to flow from *The Original Radio Scripts* and leave the double digit plus numbers flapping and gasping in the mud:

Fit the First

- 53 is the number of extra things to do when getting more from zero gravity
- 15 years is the length of time Ford Prefect had been stranded on Earth
- 35 seconds elapse before Ford Prefect joins the story
- 12 minutes to go until the end of the Earth
- 30 tonnes is the weight a sick pachyderm able to drink more than a couple or three Pan Galactic Gargle Blasters
- 6 thousand million people hadn't glanced into the ionosphere recently
- 28 pence is the price of four packets of peanuts
- One minute and 35 seconds left until the end of the world
- 30 Altairian dollars per day is what the hitch-hiker has to see the Galaxy
- 72 hours is the time required for the refit of a Vogon spaceship
- 100 billion new worlds could be explored instead of returning to Earth (and also the number of stars in the Galaxy)

- 12 book epic of Vogon poetry is called 'My Favourite Bathtime Gurgles'

Fit the Second

- 90 million miles between the unregarded sun and the insignificant planet
- 2000 years had almost elapsed since a man had been nailed to a tree
- 10 million tourists a year visit the pretty planet of Bethselamin
- 30 seconds is about the time it will take to asphyxiate in space
- $2^{267,709}$ to one are the odds against being rescued in space (and, of course, the number of the Islington flat)
- 29 seconds elapses before being rescued
- $2^{100,000}$, $2^{75,000}$, $2^{25,000}$ and $2^{20,000}$ are the descending levels of improbability of being rescued from certain death
- 57 is the kind of sub-meson brain to make some finite improbability
- 1000 years hence is the time warp the Encyclopaedia Galactica fell through
- 10 is the number of points available for a style mark
- 1951 is the year when Fit the second will be repeated

Fit the Third

- 300 miles is the orbit altitude above Magrathea
- 5 million years is the period of time that Magrathea has been dead
- 15 seconds is left until missile impact

- 547 and 78 are part of the evasive action to escape the missiles
- 8,767,128 are the odds against missiles turning into petunias and a whale
- 50,000 is the number of times Marvin is more intelligent than Trillian
- 60 thousand Altairian dollars are being paid into Veet Voojagig's account
- 10 million years is needed to find the Ultimate Question

Fit the Fourth

- 7½ million is the number of years Deep Thought will take to compute the answer to Life, the Universe and Everything
- 75 thousand generations ago the ancestors set the programme running
- Forty two is the answer to Life, the Universe and Everything
- One million star cruisers at the command of the G'Gugvant leader
- 1000 glaciers are poised to roll in Africa

Fit the Fifth

- 10 million years three times is how long Marvin had waited
- 576,324 and 576,326 are the geo-social pages in the book's glossary
- 6,800 miles is one side of a ningi, the 3-sided bit of small change
- 576,000 years they had been propelled through time
- 100,000 is the number of black battle cruisers behind them

- £597,000,812,406.07 is the price of the book's postage and packaging

Fit the Sixth

- 30 parsecs—radius of sphere within which someone's as clever as Marvin
- 573 is the number of committee meetings that haven't discovered fire
- 2 million years is the time the race will survive and for Arthur to be born
- 10 billion people were killed on the planet used in intergalactic bar billiards
- 30 points were scored according to *The Hitch-hiker's Guide to The Galaxy*

Caecum A: The 42 Explanations

There were 23 years in which Douglas Adams might have given a definitive explanation of why he chose forty two but he kept the magic dry and never gave the entire story.

Lewis Who?

One of the earliest explanations on record followed the publication of *Life, the Universe and Everything* in 1982. The interview was with John Shirley for a science fiction magazine called, confusingly, *Heavy Metal.* Douglas Adams was asked whether a part of the *Restaurant at the End of the Universe* was a 'deliberate reference to Lewis Carroll', seeming mildly irked to be hearing about this again he emphatically corrected the interviewer before running on to answer the forty two question *unprompted*:

> 'No. It isn't actually. Lewis Carroll, curiously enough, I read when I was a little kid, and it frightened me to bits and I couldn't bear it since. A number of people keep on saying that Lewis Carroll uses forty two quite a lot and find some significance in that. But if I'd used the number thirty nine other people would have found references in other people's books for that number, and so on and so forth. As far as children's books are concerned a much stronger influence would be Winnie the Pooh. Because Milne's writing is wonder—it's easy to read and beautifully written, worth having a look at again.'

'Used' could be a very significant verb: 'if I had used thirty nine' seems to show that the Ultimate Answer did not have to be forty two.

The Un-Funniest Number

Another early interview appeared in a science fiction publication called Fantastic Films. The interview was with Ken Bussanmas, a young (he started in his early teens) American writer with whom he had worked when Douglas Adams was, for a short while, a script editor for *Dr Who.* Here Douglas Adams explains (nearly everything) in comedy writers' workshop manner:

> 'If you're a comedy writer working in numbers you use a number that's funny like 17¾ or whatever. But I thought to myself if the major joke is the answer to life, the universe and everything and it turns out to be a number, that has got to be a strong joke. If you put a weak joke in the middle of it by saying not only is it a number but it's 17¾ it slightly undermines it.
>
> 'I think the point is to have complete faith in the strong joke and put the least funny number you can think of in the middle of it. What is the most ordinary, workaday number you can find? I don't even want it to be a prime number. And I guess it mustn't even be an odd number. There is something slightly more reassuring about even numbers. So I just wanted an ordinary, workaday number and chose forty two. It's

> an unfrightening number. It's a number you could take home and show your parents.'

The two answers above as well as being the two earliest apparently recorded, are also the fullest explanations. Mr King, our old chemistry master (so old we only had fourteen elements) used to tell form 4X (and we drank Australian lager) that the longer an exam question was, then the easier it should be for us to think up a feasible answer. A corollary of this would be that a long answer indicates a tricky question. Delivered some six and seven years post-script, Douglas Adams a) emphatically denies a Lewis Carroll connection, and b) specifically explains how a number can be considered an unfunny one (not the funniest number of later belief). Neither explanation is complete, lacking the detail needed to say why any other even, non-prime, workaday, whole number couldn't claim to be as unfunny as forty two and as deserving of meeting your parents. Several hundred out of ten for dissembling though—the suggested re-reading of Winnie the Pooh and the meet-the-parents joke could both be considered elegant and polite means of deflecting a conversation possibly heading towards any probing supplementary question.

No. It Doesn't Mean Anything

The Original Radio Scripts by Douglas Adams—with a faint billing for John Lloyd—had additional notes by Geoffrey Perkins, producer of all but the first episode of the radio series and a friend of Douglas Adams. The book includes comments from Douglas Adams.

Many people have asked whether the choice of forty two as the Ultimate Answer came from Lewis Carroll or perhaps from an ancient Tibetan mystical cult where it is the symbol of truth.

'In fact it was simply chosen because it was a completely ordinary number, a number not only divisible by two but also by six and seven, in fact it's the sort of number that you could without any fear, introduce to your parents.' (DA)

But a learned letter in the *New Scientist* suggested that Deep Thought may well have been right since forty two is the atomic number of Molybedenum — a chemical that could have been vital in organic life. Even more importantly the Answer gave its number to a rock group (Level 42, not UB40).

The footnote after Fit the Sixth, the last part of the original radio series, adds:

Some would-be clever people wrote in to point out that six times nine actually equals fifty four and didn't we know how to do elementary mathematics? Some would-be even cleverer people wrote in to point out that six times nine does indeed equal forty-two if calculated in base thirteen. (What no-one has spotted is that if you play a part of one of the episodes

> backwards you'll hear Bob Dylan explaining just what's gone wrong with Paul McCartney's career).

Douglas Adams further dismissed this idea by saying 'I may be a sad case but I don't write jokes in base thirteen'. Fit the Sixth was co-authored with John Lloyd as they faced the ultimate deadline, and so the six times nine section, getting numbers from Scrabble letters on the next-to-last page might have been written at a time when the writers may just have started to consider it might be appropriate to think about having the script in the post to get to the pub before last orders.

no, No, NO. It Really Doesn't Mean Anything

Douglas Adams, posted a mildy terse reply in 1993 from Sante Fe, New Mexico where he was working on the script for the film (and somewhere Dirk Gently was to be in the unfinished *The Salmon of Doubt*) as follows in an online discussion at alt.fan.douglas.adams:

> 'The answer to this is very simple. It was a joke. It had to be a small number, and an ordinary smallish number, and I chose that one. Binary representations, base thirteen, Tibetan monks are all complete nonsense. I sat at my desk, stared into the garden and thought '42 will do'. I typed it out. End of story.'

The 42 Puzzle

The growing independent life of the forty two phenomenon interested Douglas Adams enough to develop the 42 Puzzle for publication in an illustrated edition published in 1994, the year his daughter was born and in which he had his 42nd birthday. The US edition was priced at forty two dollars and Douglas Adams explained the puzzle's *raison d'être* as follows:

> '*Everybody was looking for hidden meanings* [my italics] and puzzles and significances in what I had written (like 'is it significant that 6 times 9 is 42 in base 13?'. As if.) So I thought that just for a change I would actually construct a puzzle and see how many people solved it. Of course, nobody paid it any attention. I think that's terribly significant.'

Or, 'On My Way to Work One Morning...'

This was the last or one of the last occasions (January 2000) when Douglas Adams answered the question of forty two. Appearing on the BBC Radio Four show *Book Club* he said:

> '...on my way to work one morning, whilst still writing the scene, and thinking about what the actual answer should be I eventually decided that it should be something that made no sense whatsoever, a number, and a mundane one at that.'

The evidence indicates that the scene was written by a typewriter aided by Douglas Adams aided by his mother bringing cups of tea to a room in his mother and step-father's house in darkest Dorset. So a journey to work may have been a shortish time to think up a number.

The Stephen Fry Completely Obvious

On the eve of the 30th anniversary of the original broadcast of *The Hitch-hiker's Guide to The Galaxy* Douglas Adams' friend, colleague and occasional house-sitter, Stephen Fry, was interviewed for BBC News, on the March 7th 2008 and simultaneously both illuminated and tantalised by saying:

> 'Douglas told me in strictest confidence exactly why forty two. The answer is fascinating, extraordinary and when you think hard about it, completely obvious. Nonetheless amazing for that.
>
> 'Remarkable really, but sadly I cannot share it with anyone and the secret must go with me to the grave. Pity because it explains so much beyond the books. It really does explain the secret of life, the universe and everything.'

Knows words, Stephen Fry. Picking here 'why forty two', not 'what forty two means'.

As Told to John Lloyd

At the sixth Douglas Adams Memorial Lecture on March 12th 2008, John Lloyd, his friend, and co-author of episodes Five and Six of the radio series and *The Meaning of Liff* and *The Deeper Meaning of Liff* introduced a special 30th anniversary performance of scenes from *The Hitch-hiker's Guide to The Galaxy* by members of the original cast and said that Douglas had told him it was:

'The funniest of the two digit numbers.'

It was to John Lloyd whom Douglas Adams had turned with deadlines racing up for episodes five and six. Had there been some significance associated with the choice of forty two then it appears not to have been part of their discussion and plotting for where these fifty or so minutes of radio script would be headed.

Some Interesting Reads...

Apollo 13

- A Man on the Moon: The Voyages of the Apollo Astronauts, Andrew Chaikin, 1994
- Apollo 13: Lost Moon, Jim Lovell & Jeffrey Kluger, 1994

Baseball

- Maybe I'll Pitch Forever, Leroy 'Satchel' Paige and David Holman, 1963
- Baseball's Great Experiment: Jackie Robinson and His Legacy, Jules Tygiel, 2008
- Only the Ball Was White: A History of Legendary Black Players and All-Black Professional Teams, Robert Peterson, 1992

Bay of Pigs (The)

- Decision for Disaster: Betrayal at the Bay of Pigs, Grayston L. Lynch, 1998

Butch Cassidy and the Sundance Kid

- Digging Up Butch and Sundance, Anne Meadows, 1996
- The Outlaw Trail: A History of Butch Cassidy and His Wild Bunch, Charles Kelly, 1996

Centralia

- Fire underground: The Ongoing Tragedy of the Centralia Mine Fire, David DeKok, 2009 (revised edition)

Chuck Yeager

- Yeager: An Autobiography, Chuck Yeager and Leo Lanos, 1985

Cricket

- The Don: The Definitive Biography of Sir Donald Bradman, Roland Perry, 2000 (new edition)
- The Best of the Best: A New Look at the Great Cricketers and Their Changing Times, Charles Davis, 2000
- All-Round Genius. The Unknown Story of Britain's Greatest Sportsman, Mick Collins, 2006
- In Quest of the Ashes, Douglas Jardine and Fianach Jardine, 2005 (new edition)
- Harold Larwood, Duncan Hamilton, 2009

Douglas Adams

- Don't Panic, Douglas Adams & The Hitchhiker's Guide to The Galaxy, Neil Gaiman, 2009 (revised edition)
- The Hitch-hiker's Guide to the Galaxy The Original Radio Scripts, Douglas Adams (edited and introduced by Geoffrey Perkins), 2003 (updated edition)
- Wish You Were Here: The Official Biography of Douglas Adams, Nick Webb, 2003

$E = mc^2$

- Why Does $E=mc^2$?: (and Why Should We Care?), Brian Cox, and Jeff Forshaw, 2009

Edward Whymper

- Travels Amongst The Great Andes Of The Equator With Supplementary Appendix, Edward Whymper, 1891

Groundhog Day

- Groundhog Day, Don Yoder, 2003

Gutenberg Bible (The)

- The Gutenberg Revolution: How Printing Changed the Course of History, John Man, 2009

Jack Warner

- Clown Prince of Hollywood: The Antic Life and Times of Jack L. Warner, Bob Thomas, 1990

Lewis Carroll

- Lewis Carroll in Numberland, Robin Wilson, 2008

Makin Island

- Forgotten Raiders of '42, Tripp Wiles, 2007

Oceans

- Mapping the Deep, The Extraordinary Story of Ocean Science, Robert Kunzig, 2000

Organised Crime

- Me and My Brothers: Inside the Kray Empire, Charles Kray and Robin McGibbon, 2005 (2nd Edition)
- World Encyclopedia of Organized Crime, Jay Robert Nash, 1995 (new edition)

Roadlit

- On the Road, Jack Kerouac, 1951

Statistics

- The Wisdom of Crowds: Why the Many Are Smarter Than The Few, James Surowiecki, 2005 (new edition)

Skunk Works

- Skunk Works, Ben R Rich and Leo Janos, 1995

SS Sultana

- Sultana: Surviving the Civil War, Prison, and the Worst Maritime Disaster in American History, Alan Huffman, 2009

Stanley and Livingstone

- Into Africa. The Dramatic Retelling of the Stanley-Livingstone Story, Martin Dugard, 2003
- Stanley. The Impossible Life of Africa's Greatest Explorer, Tim Jeal, 2007

Star Trek

- The Nitpicker's Guide for Classic Trekkers, Phil Farrand, 1994

Whaling (The Whaleship Essex)

- In the Heart of the Sea: The Tragedy of the Whaleship Essex, 2001, Nathaniel Philbrick

Acknowledgements

I would very much like to thank everyone who has helped and inspired me: including Fred Bermingham McDonogh and Deirdre nic Mhurchú—roast grouse, Irish house claret & wisdom; Eleanor Gill, Cesca Gill, Phoebe Gill, Milla Gill and Sebastian Broster—help in eating 42 Happy Meals (a day to remember); Ken and Susan Tonkin, John and Jacqui Wynn Jones, Barrie Spears, Stuart and Rose Crocker, Alan and Julie Otter, Bill and Amanda Gowans, Nigel and Dinah Mike, Paddy and Anne Nagel, Sue and David Groves, Ian and Julie Baguley, David and Helen Kent, Paul and Sabina Attard, Rick and Gill Liver, David and Jane Errington, Roger and Leslie Hall, George and Fiona Chancellor—all for friendship and stimulating ideas. Professor Jeff Forshaw of the Manchester University School of Physics & Astronomy, Michael Farr of Delmar Printers, and Caroline James—for special expertise. Simon, Derry, James and Roy—the no-folk-in-Ikea quiz team, and Dean and the other irregulars at the Coach & Horses.

My special thanks naturally goes to Simon Petherick, Tamsin Griffiths and Robert Pereno at Beautiful Books, for their kindness, belief, and knowledge. Also my special thanks to

Ken Welsh, for very kindly allowing me the use of his letter.

With special gratitude I would like to thank my parents, and Hannah for her infinite support and patience over 33 years—and doubly so since the day 'writing a book' joined an improbable list of other displacement activities that have resulted in the raw neglect of lawns needing mowing, things needing decorating, and the finding out of whether third-time-lucky applies to putting a shelf up.

The Big Wiki Thankyou

The book would not have been written without Wikipedia and Google. In recognition of the vital service being provided by Wikipedia two Altairian cents* will be given to the Wikipedia Foundation for every book sold.

*The Altairian dollar (ALD) is currently trading at parity or 'as near as makes no difference' with the British pound (GBP). This neatly makes the author's donation to the Wikipedia Foundation a round two pence per book.

Errors and omissions

1.

2.

3.

5.

6.

When you have six please use a separate sheet of paper.

Index

About the Author

Peter Gill was born in England and educated in Longridge, Blackburn and Reading—from where he went to Oxford but left early when he realised there wasn't quite enough of interest to sustain a full weekend. On the occasions when work has troubled his day he has conveyed the impression of being a research scientist, radio journalist, college lecturer, something in IT, PR drone, and itinerant sheep shearer.

Extirpated from his native Lancashire he now lives in a Shropshire home, accompanied by one wife, up to four daughters, a cat, the F dog, five chickens and six goldfish. He has promised never, ever, to try and keep stick insects again. His time is largely divided between the kitchen and a room on the top floor with a handy bolt on the outside.

Peter was third by one quarter of an inch in the Coach and Horses longest runner bean competition (his bean, not personally), and *42: Douglas Adams' Amazingly Accurate Answer to Life, the Universe and Everything* is his first book if you're not counting the pamphlet on electric fencing.